This copy of *WORDSMITH CRAFTSMAN* belongs to

Name: _____

Date: _____

Copyright 1996, 2003 by J. B. Cheaney
Published by **DGC** Inc., Bolivar, Missouri
Distributed by Common Sense Press, Melrose, Florida

Janie B. Cheaney taught her two children at home for twelve years, during which she also conducted creative writing classes for other homeschool students. Since 1990 she has seen her work published in magazines and literary journals. In addition she has worked with students in theater design and performance, and has written several plays for young people. Her first novel, *The Playmaker*, was published by Random House in 2000, followed by *The True Prince* in 2002. Mrs. Cheaney lives in the Ozarks of Missouri with her husband.

TABLE OF CONTENTS

TO THE TEACHER

The *Wordsmith* Philosophy

This book is the third and last of the *Wordsmith* series, and like the other two it is written with a specific goal in mind. *Wordsmith Apprentice* (for 4th-6th grades) is designed to awaken children to the varieties, possibilities, and fun of writing. *Wordsmith: A Creative Writing Course for Young People* addresses youngsters at the classic age of introspection (junior high) and helps them use their own experience as material for effective self-expression. With *Wordsmith Craftsman* the student learns to branch out, using writing skills for communication, organization and reasoning.

This book is targeted for the age group known as "young adult." In practical terms, this means high school, although the subject matter in Part Three is applicable to college age. In fact, a student who successfully completes the course should be at the skill level of a college sophomore--or beyond!

Wordsmith Craftsman assumes that the student has a working knowledge of grammar and mechanics. If this is not the case, I would suggest that you take a few months to work through a good English grammar program, or review the major points in a handbook. Also, a student beginning this book should feel somewhat comfortable about writing (even if he doesn't like it). If your 10th-12th grader is negative toward the subject, you might consider working through *Wordsmith* first. The exercises and assignments in that book are specifically designed to help a word-shy teenager develop confidence about the writing process. Without that confidence, *Wordsmith Craftsman* may be daunting.

The Structure of *Wordsmith Craftsman:*

Part One immerses the student in practical, everyday writing of the sort that we all should do. You will notice that some basic study skills are addressed here, such as note-taking and summarizing. I can't overemphasize the importance of these skills. If the student has already learned them, the extra practice in this book will help refine the technique; if not, be sure your student has mastered them before moving on to Part Two.

Part Two offers an opportunity to brush up on the mechanics of language and polish some technical skills. An in-depth study of the paragraph comprises the main part of this section, with emphases on organization, purpose, and writing style. The exercises are intended to help the student *think* about what he's doing and make conscious choices for the best effect.

In **Part Three**, it all comes together with formal essay writing. "Essay" is a dry word to most of us, associated with dusty collections of Emerson and Marcus Aurelius on the library shelf. Yet even today, in our cyber-dominated world, essays are considered the ultimate test of a writer's ability. To conceive an idea, to develop logical consequences or analogies, to construct a framework and communicate ideas effectively are the prime goals of writing: all come together in the essay. It's no exaggeration to say that a well-written essay is the mark of an educated man or woman.

At the end of Part Three, the student is expected to write eight additional essays for practice. He or she should be warned that the last page doesn't exactly mean the end!

Doing Your Part

Wordsmith Craftsman is self-teaching. Your job is to see that the work gets done and to serve as a resource guide and "reader's response" (the one who reviews the work in progress and makes helpful suggestions). From the very first page the student is expected to take charge of his assignments and schedule them within the given time limits. This may be difficult for some young people, especially if they are accustomed to having their assignments handed to them. It may be advisable for you to check the student's plan book periodically until you are confident that he is capable of scheduling realistically and following through.

You should also be the one to determine how much of the book to cover in one year. You can (and should!) be flexible, adjusting the pace to your student's abilities. In general terms, however, here's a suggested schedule:

IF YOU ARE STARTING *WORDSMITH CRAFTSMAN* IN...	PLAN TO COVER....	SKILLS:
9th Grade	First year: Part One PLUS review lessons from *Wordsmith* Second Year: Part Two Part Three, pp. 52-66 Third Year: Part Three, pp. 67-97, One research paper Fourth Year: Review Part Three One or two research papers	Notes, summaries and letter writing Further writing projects from *Wordsmith* Writing style and Descriptive and narrative essays Expository and persuasive essays, Research techniques Practice on all five essay types; Logical thought development
10th Grade	First Year: Parts One and Two Second Year: Part Three pp. 52-77, One research paper Third Year: Part Three review, pp. 78-97, one research paper	(See above)
11th Grade	First Year: Parts One, Two and Three Second Year: Part Three review One-two research papers	(See above)
12th Grade	Parts One, Two and Three One research paper	(See above)

The student will need a spiral notebook for practice, exercises and rough drafts, plus some sort of assignment book or appointment calendar. Other resources, such as back issues of *Reader's Digest* and editorial pages from the newspaper, are not hard to come by;

just be prepared. Finally, if you don't have a thesaurus, please consider buying one. Good paperback editions are available for $10 or less at most book stores: a modest investment that will pay off in word power!

If you see to it that your student faithfully follows the instructions in this book and does not skimp on practice, you can expect a young adult who is able to organize and classify ideas, write letters to suit any occasion, analyze the structure and effectiveness of everyday written material, and generate, organize and express original ideas. The results will be well worth the effort he or she invests in the challenge of learning to write.

TO THE STUDENT

These days, it's not unusual to hear someone wondering about "the future of the written word." With so much visual imagery invading our minds (TV, video, DVD, etc.), who knows if anyone will have the time or inclination to *read* in another fifty years?

If reading and writing disappear, we may as well go back to subsistence farming: civilization will be over. Do you imagine that the highly technical information our society requires can be communicated in pictures? Should we start practicing facial expressions as the best way to get our feelings across? Most of all, can we pass on ideas without the use of words?

But wait (you may be thinking); no one said anything about the disappearance of the *spoken* word. Ideas and feelings can still be expressed, just maybe not as much on paper as in earlier times.

Of course the spoken word will not disappear. In fact, spoken words are multiplying exponentially everywhere we turn--take talk radio as a case in point. But when we take the time to *listen* to what is being said, we realize that most of it is hardly worth saying. I'm not talking about the ordinary conversations that make up our relationships. I'm talking about much of what passes (on TV, radio and the Internet) for the communication of ideas. Consider a typical talk-radio exchange:

Caller: I just feel that . . . abortion isn't right. It's killing . . . uh . . .
Talk-show guest: Killing what? It's *potential* human life: a mass of tissue. Not actual human life.
Caller: But . . . but . . . I just feel . . .

Chances are the caller never tried to put her "feelings" in writing. Good writing demands complete sentences and a logical thought process. It demands some form of reasoning, not just emotion, even though emotion may take part. Writing is a conscious effort to organize ideas, choose the right words, uncover facts, consider alternatives, and present conclusions in a readable form that others can understand. At its highest level, writing is a form of thinking.

The need for this high-level mental exercise is not going away. In fact, the demand for clear communication is increasing, just as the number of people able to communicate clearly seems to be *de*creasing. We're approaching a time when writing and thinking skills will be at a premium. The goal of this book is to help you develop skill and confidence in both.

Here's an extravagant claim: Nothing you learn in your entire academic career will be more valuable to you than what you learn between these covers. I'm speaking of "head knowledge," not character development, which is a different sort of learning. All the same I hope you're impressed!

You will be responsible for making your assignments and seeing them through. Some assignments can be completed in half an hour; others will take weeks. You will think through your own schedule, determining how much time to allot for a task and when to move on to the next step. At any point where you're unsure what to do, don't hesitate to ask your teacher or parent for help. But ultimately, the responsibility is yours. That's not so bad, you know. Most endeavors become more interesting when you take charge of them yourself.

I can promise that you won't regret it.

PART ONE: WRITING EVERY DAY

When primitive cultures are introduced to writing, they often regard it as magic. How can information and ideas be passed on without one person speaking to another? In a sense, the impression of writing as miraculous is correct. Through writing, you and I communicate to individuals near at hand, or far away, or not yet born. The capacity for written language is a gift that humans should never take for granted.

In Part One of this book, we'll practice some basic forms of written communication. Some of these may not be new to you, but the practice is important. Notes, outlines, and letters are forms of writing you can expect to do for the rest of your life. Learn to do them well, and your life may go just a little easier.

TAKE A NOTE

Before beginning any task, it's necessary to gather the tools. For a writer, the most obvious tools are a pencil and clean paper, but that's not all. Other tools are less evident: ideas, information, knowledge, thought--or all four. These mental tools don't always spring readily to mind. Have you ever had the experience of staring at a blank piece of paper while the minutes crawled by like snails? Nothing seemed to happen inside your head except one monotonous thought: I can't think of *anything* to write about! Even professionals know what that's like. It's called "writer's block."

This book should help you get over writer's block in a number of ways. The first way is so simple and practical that you may never have connected it with "writing." This is the practice of making notes to yourself, including lists of things to do.

Do you know anyone who makes notes and to-do lists? These people set themselves up for a lot of teasing (good-natured or not) because they are *so organized* they make the rest of us look like slobs. In order to keep from *feeling* like slobs, we may tell ourselves, "Well, she (or he) may get a lot more done, but I'll bet she doesn't have much fun. I like to take advantage of opportunities as they come up, and you can't do that if you're tied to a list. Besides, I don't have the time."

Like it or not, we all have an increasing number of things to do and remember; that is part of being an adult. Every successful student learns to organize his or her time to accommodate school assignments, part-time work, chores, club meetings, volunteer service--both the "have tos" and the "want tos." It's true that some people are more naturally inclined toward note-jotting and list-making than others. But the discipline is worthwhile for all, no matter what their natural inclinations. Consider--

1) Listmakers *do* get more done. Not only that, but a list can save money as well as time.

2) Those who are naturally inclined to listmaking may seem less spontaneous (that is, open

to changing plans at the last minute) than those who don't make plans. On the other hand, the people who make lists are often the ones who make things happen!

3) Making a list doesn't make you a slave. Just the opposite--when you write things down, *you* are the one in charge. If unforeseen circumstances arise, you may consciously decide to skip or postpone an item. You are neither at the mercy of the list (which is *your* creation, after all) nor of your memory (which may fail you).

4) To claim that you don't have time to write things down doesn't make sense. Listmakers have *more* time, because they organize it better.

Making notes and to-do lists will help you create free time that's really free--time you can enjoy without the thought of undone responsibilities hanging over your head.

HOW TO MAKE NOTES AND TO-DO LISTS

STEP ONE. Buy a small memo book or appointment calendar. This will be your **plan book**. Since you will use it to schedule writing assignments, some sort of calendar works best. If you use a memo pad, take a few moments to label each page as a separate week: "Sept. 4-10," "Sept. 11-17," "Sept. 18- 24," etc.

STEP TWO. Keep the plan book in a handy place (such as your desk top) with a pen or pencil nearby.

STEP THREE. Write in it! Jot down: commitments when you make them ("Meet S. at Mall 2 p.m. Sat.); instructions from your parents ("Clean out garage Fri. a.m."); thoughts that come to you ("Thank Grandma for book." "Ask B. about tickets"). Write down long-range commitments and plans as well, such as spring break or the yards you contracted to mow every three weeks. HINT: keep a pen with you at all times, along with scratch paper to jot down thoughts and reminders the moment they occur to you. Regularly transfer these notes to your plan book.

STEP FOUR. Review your plan book daily. Lists and notes are no good if you forget to look at them! A quick review every morning should be enough to help keep in mind what needs to be done. As you complete items, you can cross them off the list (this is the fun part). If something doesn't get done, move it to the next day, or next convenient time, so it's not forgotten.

NOTE: Throughout this course I will be referring to your "plan book" and your "notebook." These are not the same! You will use an ordinary spiral-bound **notebook** for writing exercises, preliminary work, outlines and rough drafts. The **plan book** is for writing down what you need to do and when. You will be scheduling your own assignments within a given time frame. When you see a boxed paragraph, it's an assignment or exercise. It's also a signal to get out your plan book and make a note to yourself about when to do it.

> ASSIGNMENT. If you are using a memo book for your planning, mark a section for each day of the week. Write down all the chores, appointments, meetings and fun things you plan to do each day this week. Anticipate any preparations you will need to make, and write them under the appropriate days. For instance, if you have a presentation to give during Speech class on Thursday, make a note to yourself to "gather stuff for pres. at Speech" on Tuesday.

Follow this procedure at the start of every week for the next six months. By the end of that time, it should be a habit.

The next assignment will require some thought. Complete it within two weeks. Schedule it in your plan book NOW.

> ASSIGNMENT. In your notebook, make lists of your goals for the next year, the next five years and the next ten years of your life. One of the most outstanding traits of successful people--no matter how their success is measured--is that they set goals for themselves. Having a goal gives you a direction and a target.
>
> Your goals for this year should be realistic, specific, and not too routine. Eating breakfast every morning does not qualify as a goal! The list should include items that depend mostly on you and require at least a little work.
>
> The farther you project into the future, the hazier your goals are likely to be. "Become an artist" or "Own a business" may be an appropriate direction for you, but it's too early to work out the details. Even a general direction, however, can motivate you to take steps now, such as signing up for watercolor lessons or starting a savings account.

STUDY NOTES AND OUTLINES

If you looked up the word "note" in the dictionary, how many definitions might you find? A brief message, a single musical pitch, a reminder to yourself, a jarring instant (as in, "He struck a wrong note with his remark") are all "notes." The kind of "note" we will discuss in this section is a piece of information written in a shortened form. It is a reminder of an idea. The to-do notes were reminders from you, to you. Now we will consider notes from sources outside yourself, both written and spoken.

Picture yourself in the middle of a lecture on Plato during Philosophy 101 class. Your head nods as the instructor drones on: "The essential question of *The Republic* is, 'What is justice?' The Sophists claim that since strength is the ultimate virtue, then justice is whatever serves power. Socrates rejects this without much argument, but goes on to qualify justice as an attribute of groups, not individuals. Therefore, in order to understand what a just *man* is we must define a just *society* . . ." Sitting at your desk, you have two choices. You can doodle in your notebook, vaguely wondering why we're talking about Socrates when the lecture is supposed to be about Plato. *Or* you could try to actually learn something. It's up to you, but as long as you are spending time in this class, you may as well get something out of it. The way you learn is by taking notes.

When taking notes you must ask questions continually.   Sometimes questions have to do with facts: Who, What, Where, When and How. At other times the questions are aimed at specific concepts or ideas: Where is the author (or speaker) going with this? Why introduce this idea now? How does it relate to the previous idea? You should be asking questions at the same time that you're getting answers, all the while organizing information and writing it down. We're talking about high-level thinking here, the kind of thinking that may at first seem out of your league.

But all skills improve with practice--really. And the skill of taking notes is so basic to learning *any* academic subject that there's almost no point in continuing your education unless you can master this. Don't despair! By following the instructions in this book you will learn to do just that.

GETTING READY

Note-taking is the process of mentally organizing the material you hear or read. You can't simply copy it; you have to sort, sift, and categorize to determine what is important, even *before* writing it down. This sounds harder than it actually is. We all know how to organize, or else we would have a hard time getting through the day. I can prove it with the following exercise.

> EXERCISE. Open your notebook to a clean page and "take notes" on what you did yesterday, including both general activities and details. You will probably find yourself organizing chronologically. Try to fill up at least half a page and show some pattern of arrangement (such as indenting details under a broad heading). Use any abbreviations that you can understand.

Your "notes" should look something like this:

```
Morning routine
     get up--7:00
     bathroom--brush teeth, comb hair, shower
     stretches
     breakfast--scr. eggs and toast
School
     finish alg. assn.
     discuss research project
Lunch--12:15 (fried rice)
Chem class--1:30
     ph testing
     concocted potion with Tim
B-ball practice--3:30
     3-pt shot in 3rd 1/4!!!!
     (Josh sprained ankle)
     jogging
Dinner--6:30 (meat loaf)
Evening
```

```
finished Call of the Wild
research on science project
on-line 8:30-10:00
        played Speed trap with Shyra
        Explorer chat room--Jerrod (AK), Mariah (NM)
Bed--10:45
```

The events in this "typical day" fall into a natural order. Some details are worth including--the 3-pt shot during b-ball practice, for instance. Most are left out. It's not necessary to list what everybody wore or how you arrived at the chemistry class or how many algebra problems were incorrect. These things are all routine, pretty much the same from day to day. The point in taking notes is to outline the overall picture while catching the outstanding details.

> EXERCISE. Pretend you have to make a speech about how to perform an activity you know how to do. It might be a job, game, or special skill you've learned--anything that can be explained in *words*, not pictures or gestures.
>
> Your proposed speech will probably outline a series of steps necessary for this activity. Organize the steps in a logical manner that won't confuse your listeners, then list the steps in order, just as you listed the events of your day. If certain details occur to you after you have passed that place on your notes, feel free to go back and squeeze them in (it's a good idea to leave spaces here and there when taking notes). Leave out information that your imagined hearers would already know. Be sure to define all technical terms and include an interesting example or anecdote from your own experience.

You will soon be taking systematic notes from a written source. Before you do, you may wish to set up a little abbreviation system to help you write quickly. Some abbreviations are commonly used, such as these examples:

w/ - with	$\therefore$ - therefore	esp. - especially
w/o - without	Δ - change	i.e.- in other words
re - about (regarding)	cd, shd, wd -	nec. - necessary
$\sim$ - about (approximately)	could, should, would	e.g. - for example

Over time, you may wish to develop your own abbreviation system for words you find yourself using often. Make a list on the inside front cover of your notebook, including the abbreviations above as well as others for words that occur frequently.

In addition, you will probably devise quick, on-the-spot abbreviations for words pertaining to a particular area of knowledge, such as

Wsh--Washington	Na--Sodium
Ir.--Ireland	fibr--fibrillation

Devising abbreviations on the spot is perfectly all right, as long as you remember what those funny little two- and three-letter words mean. You will probably invent these abbreviations while writing your notes, but be sure to jot down the "translation" before you forget, or else you may be faced with something like "const pressr on v may cs serious dsequb & lead to expl."

HOW TO TAKE NOTES

On page 99 you will find a form entitled "Notes about _____". There are two ways to use this handy tool. You may wish to make several photocopies and take your notes directly on them. Or you may open this book to the form and keep it nearby as a guide while you write in a notebook.

> ASSIGNMENT. Take notes from a non-fiction source no more than four pages long (such as a book chapter or magazine article). See below for instructions on how to do this.

Your teacher may want to assign some particular reading--be sure to ask. When you have chosen your selection, follow this procedure.

STEP ONE: Write the appropriate title, author and page numbers in the top lines on the form, or on the top lines of your notebook paper. Skim the passage, noting picture captions, bold type, chapter or section headings, and any words or phrases that seem to be repeated frequently. Now you're ready to begin.

STEP TWO: When taking notes, you should include
     a. Specific information you don't already know
     b. Details that are especially interesting or have particular consequences
     c. Items, words, and concepts that the author emphasizes
     d. Important names, dates, places and technical terms
     e. Diagrams that help you understand.
     f. Questions about anything unclear to you

The space on the right side of the paper is for you to jot down any personal reactions you may have to the selection. Such reactions might be, "great stuff!" "disagree," "Who does he think he's kidding?" "Share with mom," or "I don't get it." If you are paying attention while you read, you will probably respond in some way. Such observations can help you get involved and jog your memory when you review later. By placing them in the right margin (or possibly the left, if you are using a notebook), you avoid the task of untangling your own ideas from those of your source.

STEP THREE: After you've finished your notes, take a moment to write two or three sentences at the top of the page, expressing the main ideas of the passage as you understand it. Don't neglect this step! Nothing will help you more to clarify your own thoughts or to get up to speed when reviewing the notes. Make sure you've listed any special abbreviations, then put the notes aside.

STEP FOUR: The next day, review your notes, then use them to reconstruct v
read. Pretend you are a teacher lecturing from the notes to a phantom "class" (
person, if you can find one willing to listen). If you are able to "teach" a lesson on this
subject, congratulate yourself on a job well done. If not, try again. Get another copy of the
form (or turn the page in your notebook) and reread the guidelines and the passage. Try a
little harder to make sure that your notes cover the entire range of the material.

If you develop this procedure so that it becomes automatic, you will be amazed at
how your learning capacity is increased.

> Over the next two weeks, take notes at least three times per week from your
> assigned reading. Review the previous four steps each time until the procedure is
> set in your mind. In your plan book, schedule days to take notes. Do it *now.*

> Practice this system of taking notes at least twice per week throughout the school
> year--for instance, every Monday and Thursday. Schedule this in your plan book
> *now!* (If unforeseen complications pop up, you can always reschedule.)

ORAL SOURCES

Now it's time to move on to taking notes from an oral source: a lecture, TV documentary,
or any other type of spoken presentation. This is more challenging, as you do not have the
luxury of time to reread a difficult section or get a glass of water. You must be mentally
"on your toes" as long as the speaker is speaking--constantly sorting, classifying, or
categorizing the information coming at you.

"Staying mentally on your toes" is not a cute metaphor; it's an absolute necessity.
Below are two effective techniques for listening. Choose the technique that suits you.

a. **Anticipate what the speaker will say next**. This amounts to carrying on an internal
dialogue with yourself as both student and interpreter. The student part of you writes
busily while the interpreter leads the way with unspoken comments, such as, "I'll bet
she starts criticizing Republicans now"; "That's the second time he's repeated that
phrase--it must be important"; "He's about to explain the underlying causes of the war";
"Now she's building up to a conclusion--I hope." The speaker may surprise the
interpreter in you by taking a turn you didn't expect, but if you are this involved in the
lecture, it won't take you long to catch up.
b. **Ask questions**. This approach is very similar to the previous one, except that here the
dialogue (though still unspoken) is with the speaker. "What does 'recombinant' mean?"
"But why did Jefferson change 'pursuit of property' to 'pursuit of happiness'?" "What
were some other causes of the Great Depression?" "Where are you coming from" (i.e.,
what's your underlying point of view)? When you ask questions you will find yourself
listening for answers.

As you take notes, keep these pointers in mind:

1. **Indicate subordinate ideas by indenting them under the main idea.** A rough pattern of organization should appear shortly after the presentation begins. By five or ten minutes, you should have some idea where the talk is headed. If you don't, it may not be your fault. Some speakers either don't organize well to begin with, or they don't stick to the point. This makes it harder for you, of course, but you must persevere in writing down anything that seems important. After the presentation is concluded, the pattern (provided there *is* a pattern) may come into focus for you.

2. **Write down definitions, emphasized (or repeated) words, diagrams or terms written on a blackboard, statements introduced with ordering phrases such as "First of all," "The second point is," "Finally," etc.** You can omit general information, certain examples (or indicate them with a few words), personal anecdotes, asides to people in the audience, and most of the picky details or statistics that support secondary points.

3. Your personal responses will be limited to one or two words, such as "look this up," "yeah!," "ask Dr. P.," or "?" **Be sure to indicate any parts you don't understand.** If you are allowed to interrupt with a question, do so; if not, you may be able to ask the speaker or look it up later.

Ready? Make sure your pencil is as sharp as your mind--two pencils are better than one--and prepare yourself to listen.

> Take notes from a classroom lecture, speech, or educational TV or video program. You will use the same form on page 99.

> Take notes from an oral source at least once per week for the next two months, starting next week.

How important is it to learn this? If you attend college, you will receive most of your instruction from classroom lectures, and your grades will depend on how well you absorb what the teachers say. In the workplace, you'll need to jot down instructions or comments from your supervisor or a seminar speaker. Effective note-taking is essential for future success--start learning it now!

OUTLINING

Once you've learned to take notes, outlining is a snap. An outline is a chart showing the relationship of ideas or facts on any given subject. Note-taking is a kind of rough outlining; you separate the main ideas and line up supporting or dependent ideas below them. The difference with an outline is that you take more care to show the relationships by a prescribed system of Roman numerals, Arabic numerals, and capital and lower-case letters.

The standard outline form looks like this:

```
                    TITLE
I. First Main Classification
   A. Supporting fact
   B. Supporting fact
         1. detail
         2. detail
               a. further details on the details
               b. even more details
```

Outlines are helpful when you are organizing material. We keep running across some form of that word "organize," don't we? That's because a writer can't get along without it. Few writers can even begin to set words on paper without having some organizational principle in mind. Is this too confining? Not at all! You can be as creative as you want about your organization.

> Go back to the notes you made about a day in your life. Make a formal outline of that day, but this time arrange the material in some pattern other than chronological. See the example below.

You might group items in your day from most significant to least (or vice-versa), funny to serious, have-tos to want-tos. Here's how we reorganized our example on page 4.

```
  I. Routine
     A. Morning stuff
           1. up at 7:00
           2. brush teeth, etc.
     B. School
     C. Chem class
           1. ph testing
           2. made potion with Tim
     D. Homework
           1. finished reading Call of the Wild
           2. Alg. lesson
 II. Essentials
     A. So-so meals
           1. breakfast--better if it wasn't so early
           2. lunch--fried rice again (down with sprouts!)
     B. Four-star dining
           1. Meat-lover's pizza after practice
           2. dinner--meatloaf and twice-baked potatoes
     C. Fitness
           1. stretches
           2. jogging after practice
III. Bright spots
     A. 3-point shot in b-ball
     B. Computer
           1. cliffhanger game of Speedtrap
           2. met Jerrod from Alaska in Explorer chat room
```

> Outline a trip you took within the last year or two--first chronologically, and then in a pattern other than chronological. Each outline should be about one page long.

PERSONAL LETTERS

We live in a technologically advanced society, capable of flinging words thousands of miles per minute via e-mail, or receiving clear images bounced off a satellite from the other side of the globe. And yet we still find ourselves waiting eagerly for the mail carrier. The sight of a plain old-fashioned envelope--with a cancelled stamp in one corner and our name hand-written in the center--is still exciting. We have a letter! Who's it from? What does it say?

Few of us will grow up to be reporters or novelists, but we should all be letter writers. For some occasions, nothing else will do. Telephones are priceless, but words spoken over the wires are quickly gone. Many of us like to keep in touch by e-mail, but cyberspace communication is often less than thoughtful and (unless printed and filed) almost as fleeting as a telephone conversation. Letters can say exactly what the writer wants to say, and they stick around to be read over and over. No other type of communication can fill the special place held by letters.

THANK-YOU NOTES

The first correspondence most of us tackle is the Thank-you Note. Remember your mother asking, "Haven't you written to Aunt Jean *yet?*" If you don't know how to write a memorable Thank You, it's time you learned. The basic form does not vary, whether the writer is 6, 16, or 60. Three or four sentences will suffice.

1. After your salutation ("Dear____ "), begin with "Thank you for (the specific gift you received)." (If you just say "Many thanks for the Christmas present," the gift-giver may wonder if you remember what it was!)

2. The second sentence or two should explain how you plan to use the gift. This may call for some ingenuity, but don't shy away from being specific.

3. Close with another expression of thanks or appreciation, such as, "You always know what I need." This last statement may be formal or casual, depending on how well you know the recipient of your thank-you note.

EXAMPLES:

Dear Gus,

Thanks so much for the book on
World War II Aircraft you sent
for my birthday. I've already
looked at all the pictures (at
least twice!) and they're
fascinating. I'll get into
the text this weekend. I do
appreciate your
thoughtfulness.

Sincerely,   *alex*

Dear Aunt Mary,

I was so happy to get the
gloves! The weatherman says a
cold front is moving this way,
so they'll certainly be
appreciated when we go cross-
country skiing this weekend.
You always seem to know just
what I need. Thanks so much.

Love,   *Sarah*

> Mark specific days in your plan book to write one thank-you note every month for
> the next three months (and additional notes when appropriate). You may write to
> someone who's helped you, a teacher who conducted a special class for you, or a
> parent "just because." With a little thought, you can always find someone to thank.

KEEPING IN TOUCH

The thought of a "letter" usually brings to mind the informal, chatty, 1-2 page missive that helps us keep in touch with a distant friend or relative. This is the function that e-mail has taken over, with a great advantage in speed and ease. But e-mail correspondence can be just as boring as any other kind. These suggestions will help liven up everyday correspondence.

A personal letter should sound like having a conversation with someone you haven't seen for a while. The trouble is, you will have to do all the talking. You may be a great conversationalist, but as soon as you sit down to write, you don't seem to have anything worth saying. Can you fill up an entire page with comments about the weather? What you need is source material, and to find it you turn to your own life. The letter, after all, is mostly about you; it's a way to share something of yourself.

The surest way to bore your reader is by generalizing. Compare these two letters:

Dear Pat,
     We just got back from a trip out west and it was
really fun, even though I got tired of all the driving.
We saw the Grand Canyon, the Painted Desert, the
Petrified Forest, Bryce Canyon and Carlsbad Caverns. I
think I enjoyed Bryce Canyon the most. We did lots of
hiking and some backpacking. I'm still a little sore!

When we got home our pipes were frozen. Since we left at spring break we didn't expect that cold snap, so Dad didn't weatherize anything. Most of the damage was in the basement. We spent the last day of vacation drying it out. Resting up after our vacation, ha!

Hope everything is okay with you.

Yours,

Heather

Dear Pat,

I wish you could have gone on vacation with us. The Grand Canyon was awesome, and the other sights were pretty impressive. But I liked Bryce Canyon best. We arrived on the rim just before dusk on Tuesday, and the first sight of it struck us speechless--even me! The colors were so intense. The canyon is full of rock spires that make you think of organ pipes in a <u>huge</u> cathedral. I could almost hear music. We got to spend all day Wednesday hiking the trails, and that was lots of fun. I'll never forget that first view, though. I didn't want to leave on Thursday.

We noticed something was wrong with our faucets as soon as we got home on Friday night. Dad went down to the basement to check and stepped into two inches of water! Our pipes had frozen--who would have expected a hard freeze in <u>March</u>? We spent all day Saturday mopping up. We had to throw out some of the food we had in storage, but fortunately nothing else was ruined beyond repair. "Resting up after our vacation"--ha!

Hope you all got over the flu. Have you seen any wild geese yet?

Yours,

Heather

Even though it's longer, the second letter is more interesting, both to read *and* to write. Summary sentences and paragraphs are useful in their place, but the appeal of a letter is in the details.

Your closing paragraph should be directed toward the recipient of the letter--this is supposed to be a conversation, after all. Comment on something the two of you hold in common, or ask a question about your friend's activities or thoughts. A provocative question may even inspire your correspondent to write back.

You now know some simple rules for writing an informal personal letter:
1. Use a friendly tone.

2. Be specific.

3. Include your reader.

In addition, you should be aware of a few "Don'ts":

- Don't bare your soul about an issue or struggle in your life unless you are writing to a *very* close friend. To burden an acquaintance with your private woes is inappropriate. (This seems especially true about communication over the Internet, where some correspondents get up close and personal with people they've never even met. As someone said, "We're supposed to get to know each other from the outside in, not the inside out." In other words, friendships should begin on a casual level before they burrow deep.)
- Don't tell secrets about mutual acquaintances, just because your reader is distant and "won't pass it on." Gossip is gossip, no matter what the results.
- Don't ramble on about yourself. Sprinkle brief questions and comments throughout the letter to show you're aware of your reader, and try to make the letter interesting to him or her.

Think of someone you can write. If all your friends and relatives are nearby, then find the address of that kid you met in camp last summer. If you've lost every address anyone ever gave you, then choose someone in the area whom you've not seen for a few weeks or months--an elderly friend or an acquaintance who's been sick. One way or another, *find someone to write.*

Look over the list below. Choose three or four of the topics, and write at least one paragraph on each. Some of the topics may get out of hand and take up more than one paragraph, but that's all right--you'll just end up with a *long* letter. Although you should be as neat as possible, it's permissible in an informal letter to abbreviate words, cross out a few words or phrases, or add afterthoughts in the margins--as long as it's all readable. You may also use **colloquial** (conversational) terms, such as "Oh, well," "Yeah," or "See ya!"

Letter topics:

something you learned to do recently
any change, small or large, in your life
  over the last few months
an amusing incident the last few months
an interesting dinner conversation
a trip or excursion
a problem you solved

an interesting thought that occurred to
 you
a school struggle
a new friend or acquaintance
a school triumph
a great book you read recently (and what
 you liked about it)

> Write a personal letter, one or two pages in length, to a friend or relative. If you don't know what to write about, follow suggestions above.

> Following the same guidelines, write another personal letter every month for the next three months.

THE FAN LETTER

Have you ever been so deeply affected by a book that you wanted to tell the author how you felt? Is there someone in public life--a sports star, a political figure, a crusader--whom you admire? If the thought of writing such a person ever darted through your head, you may have dismissed it because a "famous person" wouldn't be interested in anything you had to say. But you may be wrong. *Very* famous people would probably not have time to reply to your letter--or perhaps even to read it, much as they would like to. But most people who write books, fight political battles, or perform in local theater or music groups could be greatly encouraged by an enthusiastic letter from you.

> This week, write a fan letter to a person who has done something you admire. Follow the instructions and guidelines below.

Once you decide whom to write, track down the address. This may seem like a daunting task, but you don't have to go through every phone book in the U.S. Almost anyone in the public eye can be reached if you know where to look. If an Internet search doesn't yield results, try the library.

* If you are writing an author, mail your letter in care of (c/o) the publishing company. Your librarian can find the address for you.
* For someone you read about in a magazine or other publication, seal your letter (addressed with the person's name) in a stamped envelope and put it inside another envelope addressed to the magazine. Include a polite note to the magazine requesting that they forward the letter for you.
* Letters to government figures can be sent to the building where their office is located. Your local librarian can help you with this.
* People associated with a specific cause can often be reached through the organization which promotes that cause (National Right to Life, the Sierra Club, the Flat Earth Society, etc.). Most of these have a website, or ask your librarian.
* *Who's Who in America* is a book containing biographies, names, and addresses of distinguished people in every field. Most large libraries keep a reference copy.

Once you know you can reach this person, it's time to write. Since you are writing someone you don't know personally, crossouts and marginal notes are not acceptable. Write a rough draft of your letter in your notebook first. Then type it, if possible, so it will be easy to read.

1. Start with the date, then skip a line and type your recipient's name and address. Skip another line and type, "Dear Mr. (or Ms.)."

2. In the first paragraph, introduce yourself and explain how you came to know this person's work.

3. In the second paragraph, tell specifically why you admire this person's work. Include any details that "connect" you to what he or she has done. If there is anything you want to know, ask a question--but not a barrage of them.

4. In the third paragraph, express your good wishes for the recipient's further work.

5. "Sincerely" is always appropriate as a closing. Leave room to sign your name, then type your name and address beneath the signature. Most letters quickly get separated from their envelopes, and your recipient may wish to write you back.

September 4, 2002

Hon. Dick Gellum
Room 510 State Capitol
Jefferson City, Missouri 65101

Dear Mr. Gellum,

I am a junior enrolled in St. Thomas Aquinas School in Dallas County, Missouri. This fall in my government class I learned about HB 177 (the "Freedom of Private Schools Act"), which you introduced in the last legislative session.

I feel very blessed to attend a small private school, and I'm grateful to my parents for providing me with this opportunity. I realize however that we must never take these freedoms for granted. That's why I appreciate the efforts of representatives like you.

I hope to stay informed of other legislative developments in the area of education. My best wishes are with you. I hope you'll continue your fine work representing us.

Sincerely,

Peter Sanchez

Peter Sanchez
P. O. Box 78
Buffalo, MO 65622

May 17, 2003

Katherine Paterson
c/o HarperCollins
10 E. 53rd St.
New York, NY 10022

Dear Ms. Paterson,

I am a fourteen-year-old girl with a younger sister who seems to get all the breaks. A few weeks ago I was browsing the shelves of our local library when I saw the title Jacob Have I Loved. I thought it sounded interesting, so I checked out the book and took it home.

I don't know how you did it, but the story really touched my heart. My sister is so much like Caroline! And I have to admit that my feelings toward her are often much like Louise's. I think that I can understand our relationship better with the perspective you gave me. Very few stories have moved me the way that one did.

I'll be looking for other books by you. I hope you'll continue to write.

Sincerely,

Jenny Rice

Jenny Rice
120 E. Main
Janesville, OH 45729

15

The overall tone of your letter should be friendly and genuine, not flowery or flattering. Don't try to impress with your extensive vocabulary or masterful turn of phrase; just be yourself. Some other "don'ts":

- Don't allow your enthusiasm to run on for more than a page. Public figures love to hear from admirers, but their time is limited.
- Avoid extreme language, such as, "the most courageous thing I ever heard of," "the best book I ever read in my whole life," etc. Keep exclamation marks to a minimum--no more than two.
- Don't get personal, either with the information you volunteer or with your questions.

And finally, don't be surprised if you receive an answer. It may be special enough to keep for a lifetime.

> Write two more fan letters over the next two months. Schedule it now.

LETTERS OF SUPPORT

Another kind of letter, which we all have to contemplate at one time or another, is the kind that says, "I'm standing by you." A classmates's father has suddenly died, a relative is gravely ill, or a friend is having some emotional problems. When someone you know is going through a difficult time, you may want to help, but don't know how to begin. A brief letter of support may help much more than you know.

The message must come from your heart, and no one can tell you exactly what that message is. In very general terms, however, your letter should include
1. an expression of regret for the specific situation

2. a statement of how the news makes you feel

3. personal news, if it does not distract from the tone

4. a closing expression of sympathy, plus any assurance of support, prayer, or other help that you may be able to provide.

Some of the "don'ts" for this type of letter are

- Don't be trivial or decorate your letter with smiley faces or little jokes ("ha ha!")-- unless you know this person *very* well and are certain that he or she would appreciate the light touch.
- On the other hand, don't be gloomy. No matter how dark the picture, there's hope.
- Don't say, "I know how you feel." Everyone is different, and we can't presume to "feel" for each other. Also, it's usually best not to share a similar experience or problem in your family.

- Don't give advice. The letter itself should make it plain that you are available should your friend want to discuss the matter with you.

EXAMPLE:

Dear Katie,
    I was so sorry to hear about your broken ankle. I couldn't help wondering, "Why now?"--with the state track finals coming up. The disappointment must be terrible!
    I do hope you'll have a quick recovery and be back on the track soon. Next week Mom has to come into town for a doctor's appointment (we're expecting another baby!). I'll give you a call and see if there's a good time for us to come by for a visit.
                                    Love 'til then,
                                        Susan

If you do not know anyone who needs a letter of support just now, choose from the scenarios below. According to the guidelines on the previous page, write two letters of support over the next two months (that's three letters in all). Schedule this in your plan book.
    A politician whom you admire is taking an unpopular stand.
    A close relative lost his or her job.
    A friend's mother is facing life-threatening surgery .
    Your best friend's pet was run over and killed.

LETTERS OF APOLOGY

Comforting a distressed friend is hard enough, but it's even harder when *you* are the cause of the distress. You may not have meant to be so thoughtless that time you hurt your friend's feelings or upset your grandmother, but the damage has been done. Now you need to apologize. A simple "I'm sorry" may be enough, but sometimes a letter is more appropriate, especially if the injured party is not someone you see regularly. Sometimes a written apology can clear the air and restore a bruised relationship.

This is another letter you may not need to write at the moment. But sooner or later, you will blow it! How do I know that? Sooner or later, we *all* blow it.

A letter of apology need not be any longer than a paragraph. Your first step is to think about it. Be clear with yourself and determine as honestly as possible what you did wrong. Then write your salutation and follow these guidelines:

1. Start with a clear statement of how you understand the situation.

2. Follow this with an expression of your regret, which need be no more elaborate than "I'm sorry."

3. If you can think of any way to make amends, or if you have made any resolutions about your behavior in the future, be sure to mention it.

4. Close with an expression of hope that the wounded party will forgive you, and you can be friends again.

Your tone should be straightforward and honest. Avoid the following pitfalls:

- Don't make excuses for your behavior. You may have been tired, angry, or frustrated that day, but your personal feelings don't count. It's your behavior toward other people (what you *do,* not how you feel), that reveals your true character.
- Don't grovel. Most of your friends don't want to see you pour ashes on your head. Avoid exaggerations like, "I'll never forgive myself," or, "That has to be the stupidest thing anybody's ever done!" Such statements tend to put the spotlight on you, rather than on your offensive action and its effect on others.
- Don't try to be cute or funny. This trivializes the situation and makes your reader doubt your sincerity.

EXAMPLE:

```
Jeff,
     I've been regretting what I said about your test
scores ever since last Friday night.  I was trying to be
funny and "one of the guys," but as soon as the words
were out I remembered you had told me your scores in
confidence.  Just thinking how I would feel if the
tables were turned makes me cringe.  I've wished over
and over again that I could take the words back, but all
I can say is that I'm really sorry.
     At least this will teach me to think twice before
opening my big mouth.  I hope we can be friends again.

                              Sincerely,

                              Dave
```

If you haven't done anything recently for which you should apologize, choose from the scenarios below and write a "practice" apology. Don't forget to write a real one when the need arises--and mail it!
     You burned out Uncle Jakes's power drill.
     You failed to keep a commitment you made.
     You told the truth, but in a smug or unloving way.
     You accidentally hit a team member with a baseball bat.

BUSINESS LETTERS

Most jobs require written communication. Employers report that the poor language skills of their employees are becoming a problem because the demand for clear, concise writing has never been greater. Competence in writing is a precious asset, no matter what occupation you choose. Three principles govern all business writing:

1. **Respect**. At least half of all business correspondents are people you either don't know at all, or know only casually. Most are in a position to grant a request or give you some kind of assistance. Your attitude toward *every* business correspondent should be one of respect for a fellow worker doing an important job.

2. **Consideration**. Our society is busier all the time, and most working people, whether they work in the home or not, face a very full schedule every day. Your first consideration should be for their *time*. Many of the conventions for writing business letters--the return address, the typing, the brief paragraphs, even the way the letter is folded--have developed out of this concern.

3. **Clarity**. Because time is at a premium, you must be concise and very clear. Make every word count; say exactly what you need to say, and very little more.

The standard form of a business letter hasn't changed since the invention of typewriters.

All lines should begin at the left margin. On the first line, type the date.

Space down two lines and type the recipient's name (if known), the company name, and the complete business address.

Space down two more lines and type the salutation, followed by a colon (:). If you know the name of the individual, type "Dear Mr. (or Ms.):" If you know the name but are uncertain of the gender, type the entire name (e.g., "Dear Chris Sanders; Dear J.D.Ratchet:") If you don't know the name, "Dear Sir or Madam:" will cover anyone.

Leave another space and begin your letter. The first paragraph should state your purpose. Further paragraphs can elaborate.

Conclude with a brief sentence or two expressing your appreciation for their time. If you anticipate a response, say so.

"Sincerely" is always an acceptable closing.

Four lines down, type your name and address. Sign in the space between the closing and the typed address.

October 6, 2003

Italian Board of Tourism
2728 Avenue of the Americas
New York, NY 10018

Dear Sir or Madame:

My brother and I are planning a backpacking trip to Italy. We are especially interested in the Tuscan region. I would appreciate any maps, brochures or other material offered by your agency.

Thank you for your help. We look forward to hearing from you.

Sincerely,

Jason Shawcroft

Jason Shawcroft
Rt. 1, Box 14
Vermont, ID 88621

A business letter should be folded in thirds and mailed in a long envelope. Fold the paper accordion-style, with the top third bent back and the bottom third folded forward. This makes it easier for the recipient to remove the letter and shake it out for reading.

> This week, write or type two business letters requesting information. You may wish to write the College Board for information about preparing for the SAT, or write to a college or university that interests you. If you're planning a trip, state boards of tourism offer information on parks and vacation spots (check your local library or state government websites for addresses). If you'd like to engage in consumerism, most mail-order retailers send free catalogues on request.

LETTERS OF COMPLAINT

You may have had the unhappy experience of buying a product that disappointed you: some vital parts were missing, the cheap plastic gears stripped after only two months of use, or you found a roach leg in a bag of potato chips.

Of course you don't want to be a whiner, but there is a time for a legitimate complaint. Companies should be held responsible for their products; that's how our free market works. Besides, you are not a helpless victim. When you are short-changed for any reason, you have the freedom to express your disappointment.

If you are firm, clear, and respectful, most customer service departments will make an effort to satisfy you, often with free products or coupons for further services. Even if they don't, you will have the satisfaction of doing your part for the free enterprise system. Here's how to go about writing a letter of complaint:

1. If you still have the packaging, look there for the manufacturer's address. If the address is not printed, find the manufacturer's name somewhere on the product, and look up the address at the library or on the Internet. Address your complaint to the Customer Service Department, and write your salutation as "Dear Sir or Madam:."

2. In the first paragraph, tell when, where and for how much you purchased the product or service, and what you expected of it.

3. In the second paragraph, explain *precisely* why your expectations were not met. Avoid sarcasm, and be as specific as possible; your comments will help the manufacturer in addressing the problem.

4. In the third paragraph, state what sort of compensation you expect, if any. If the product comes with a guarantee (check the packaging), this is easy--you want your money back. If your complaint is about a service, you could mention that your attorney will be in touch with them (just kidding!). You may suggest that they honor their commitment to quality by returning your purchase price, or you may close with the hope that they will be more careful about quality control in the future.

EXAMPLE:

[date and address]

Dear Sir or Madam:

Last month I purchased a Light Touch scientific
calculator, Model XT-300, for $8.98 from the local
Better-Value Hardware store. I read the instructions
carefully before using it, and the calculator performed
well for more than two weeks.

Since last Friday, however, the readouts have been
unpredictable. Sometimes I get the right answer, but
over half the time I just get "8888" or a bunch of
lines. This makes geometry lessons very difficult.

My dad says it would probably cost more to fix the Light
Touch than it would to buy a new calculator. Under the
terms of your warranty I am returning the calculator
with the store receipt and requesting a refund. I don't
want the Light Touch repaired because I have already
purchased another calculator for school.

Thank you for your prompt attention.

Sincerely,

[signature, typed name, and return address]

Write a letter of complaint this week. If you have purchased a defective product
lately, write the letter about that (and mail it!). If not, use one of the scenarios
below for a practice letter.
   An appliance burned out or broke only three weeks after purchase.
   You waited over an hour for service at a local restaurant.
   You canceled your subscription to a magazine, but the company has not
      returned the balance of your subscription.
   The discount store provided an inferior substitute for an advertised item, but did
      not lower the price.

REQUESTS FOR EMPLOYMENT

Think of a business nearby where you would like to work, either as a part-time
employee or apprentice. Are you interested in gardening? computers? children? books? If
so, a greenhouse, electronics store, preschool, or library might be interested in you. Or an
attorney might choose you as an intern, or a local photographer as an apprentice. Or you
may just feel the need to earn some money. That's a need that most of us feel, eventually.

Prospective employees usually apply in person for a particular job, but a letter of introduction could help pave your way, especially if you are underage or seeking an apprenticeship. Such a letter is like a salesman making a "pitch"--the product you must sell is yourself, neatly packaged in three paragraphs.

1. Determine where and to whom you should address your request for work. Even if you don't intend to mail this letter, call the business and ask politely who is in charge of hiring. If it's a large company, ask for the name of the head of personnel. Getting the name is important because a letter addressed to an individual will usually receive more attention than one addressed to a "Dear Sir or Madam." Write the date, address and proper salutation.

2. In the first paragraph, explain what you know about this business, noting any positive impressions you've received. You might also pass on any compliments heard from others. As long as you are truthful (but not excessive), this is not flattery.

3. In the next paragraph, list your previous job experiences and any skills you've learned that will help you do this job. Enthusiasm for the product or service is also to your advantage; employers look for workers who sincerely believe in the value of what they do. Be honest and specific about any character qualities you have gained (such as punctuality, willingness, determination) that would make you an asset on the job.

4. The concluding paragraph should explain why you want to work at this particular business and what you could do to help. Close with a statement of how you intend to follow up.

EXAMPLE:

[date and address]

Dear Dr. Starr:

You may not remember meeting me, but I have been in your clinic twice with our cocker spaniel, Seymour. Both times, I appreciated the efficiency of your staff and admired your way with animals. Our neighbors, the Smithsons, have also been very pleased with your care of their rottweiler, Toby.

I have loved animals (especially dogs) ever since I can remember. Someday I hope to become a veterinarian myself. I've taken care of Seymour since he was two weeks old. In addition, I have my own pet care business--boarding animals for neighbors when they go on vacation. My business is growing because I have a reputation for being dependable. Also, I've never met a pet I didn't like!

I would very much like to work part-time in your clinic
as an apprentice. I would be willing to do anything to
help: clean out the boarding kennels, baby-sit animals
under sedation, or even file papers in the office. I
think I could ease the work load for your assistants
while I learn from watching you. I've discussed this
with my parents, and they are willing to work with you
on my schedule and see that I get to the clinic on time.

I do hope you will consider my request. I plan to call
your office on Friday the 17th to ask for an interview.

Sincerely,

[signature, name, return address]

This week, write two letters requesting employment to local businesses that could use your services.

Even if you don't plan to mail either of the letters, you might reconsider once they're finished. If you've done a good job of selling yourself, your own mother will want to hire you!

SUMMARIES

A **summary** is a concise statement of the meaning of a passage, section, chapter, or entire book. If you've ever traveled a long distance by plane you may be familiar with the term "flyover" country. This is the area you cross to reach your destination: general and unfocused, when you're 30,000 feet above it. In the same way, a written summary is a "flyover" of material you read or studied: a general landscape, with no close-ups or details.

Now I must point out an apparent contradiction. Throughout this book, and perhaps throughout your school career, you will be continually exhorted to be specific in your writing. Words like "focus," "narrow," "pointed," and "detail" will occur over and over. These words are the key to effective, interesting communication. The quickest way to lose a listener or a reader is to start talking in broad, general terms. It's the kiss of death!

But summary writing is just that--broad, general terms. What good can it be? What's the point?

Summaries are often necessary. Their use is so widespread we even have names for different types of summaries. A *brief* summarizes a law case, a *synopsis* encapsulates a fictional plot, a *resume* covers previous job experiences, and a *prospectus* outlines the outstanding features of a proposed business venture. All of them are written to communicate a broad range of information in little time. But a summary can serve other purposes as well.

1. It is an invaluable study tool. When you read a chapter in your American history text, for example, you should be comprehending not only events, places and people, but also the underlying relationships that tie them all together. To write a summary you must strip off the details and get down to the bare machinery, so to speak--the major causes that set great events in motion. This forces you to think about what is essential and what is of lesser importance; what must be included in your summary and what can be left out.

2. Summary paragraphs in a magazine or newspaper article can quickly inform the reader about material previously covered, as in this example:

> In the last installment of our "Hazardous Haste" series, Dr. Craig detailed how our "hurry-up" culture has led to countless avoidable accidents at home and on the road. Speeding is the major cause of an estimated 21% of traffic accidents. Trips and spills due to haste are the third major cause of household accidents, and ice-slippage injuries are at an all-time high. Most of these mishaps are related, at least in part, to a mindset of speed.

3. In fiction, summaries are used to "telescope" a sequence of events that are not vital to the plot of a story, but help the reader fill in the narrative gaps.

> In the two months since he had last seen Celia, Harold had foiled two counterfeiting plots, rescued an Italian diplomat from terrorists, broken an undercover gambling racket, and sat through Wagner's entire "Ring" cycle.

4. In historical writing, a summary can create the background necessary for understanding the event in question.

> To many of the American patriots preparing for the invasion, Canada was already part of the United States by right. Since 1763, when General James Wolfe defeated the French at Quebec, French Canadians had resented the Union Jack and gave every indication of wishing to be free. General Arnold expected to use this French sentiment in his favor when he sought to recapture Quebec under the American flag.

For many school assignments, you will be required to read a passage in a book, determine the main points, and summarize them in a way that shows their connection. There are two basic approaches to this task. One is to copy the key words, phrases and sentences in the original passage and connect them in a readable paragraph. The result is called an **abstract** of the original work. In the paragraph below, notice how the introduction to this book ("To The Student," p. iii) has been reduced to an abstract. The italicized words have been added for clarity and transition. Compare the original and the abstract carefully. (This is a sneaky way to get you to read the introduction if you haven't already done so.)

> These days, it's not unusual to hear someone wondering about "the future of the written word." *But* if reading and writing disappear, civilization

will be over. It's true that the spoken word will never disappear *as long as humanity remains, but writing is important for helping people clarify their thoughts. In fact,* at the highest level, writing is a form of thinking. We are approaching a time when writing and thinking skills will be at a premium. The goal of this book is to help you develop competence in both. Your responsibility is to take charge of the learning process, *but the effort will be worthwhile.* Nothing you learn *in school* will be more valuable to you.

The second and more common approach is to distill the main ideas of a passage into your own words. This is called a **précis** (pray-SEE). This method involves reducing paragraphs, pages, or even entire chapters (depending on the length of the passage you must summarize) into a single sentence. But just reducing paragraphs to the main ideas is not enough. You must also be able to show the *relationships* between the ideas; to follow the author's thought, so to speak, by making the same connections he or she has made. The paragraph below is a précis of the same introduction (p. iii):

> With all the visual imagery available these days, the importance of the written word is downplayed. But reading and writing are essential to civilization. Without it, we could not communicate information, emotions, or ideas. Of course the spoken word will continue, or even increase, but speaking does not require the same high level of thought as writing does. At a time when writing skills seem to be decreasing, the need for clear writing (and thinking) has never been greater. This book will teach those skills--but the student must take responsibility for learning them. The stakes are high: no academic skill will be more valuable than the ability to write clearly and effectively.

Summarizing is not necessarily easy, but it's well worth your time to develop. No exercise is better than summary writing for promoting both reading comprehension and thinking ability.

HOW TO WRITE A SUMMARY

On page 100 you'll find a form that will be helpful as you learn to write summaries. Make several photocopies of this form to use in future assignments. You may punch holes along the left side to keep them in a loose-leaf notebook, or tuck them into the pockets of a portfolio. As you become accustomed to writing summaries, you may discard the forms and follow a similar procedure on ordinary notebook paper.

1. Skim the passage to be summarized and get a sense of the overall meaning. Note the words that are repeated more than once--these are likely to be key words that you must understand in order to capture the meaning of the passage. Jot these words down in the designated area of the form.

2. Now read the passage more carefully. Underline (or mark with a star in the margins) any phrases or sentences that appear to sum up the author's main idea. Ask yourself questions suitable for the type of material. If history: *What were the underlying causes of*

this event? How did this cause lead to that effect? If science: *What are the technical terms that must be understood? What is the process?*

3. Mentally divide the passage into 3-6 sections. Make up a title for each section and write these titles in your notebook, or in the "General Organization" area of the form. These titles will serve as an outline for your précis.

4. This seems like a lot of preliminary work, but the preliminaries count most in summary writing. If you've completed the three previous steps you should be ready to write. Keep these guidelines in mind while writing the summary:

a. Stick to the essentials. Ideas are important here, not examples, details, descriptions, or colorful adjectives.
b. Link these ideas in a way that shows their relationship. This may mean adding sentences or phrases of your own, as in this example from the abstract paragraph on page 23: The responsibility is yours, *but the effort will be worthwhile.*
c. Write a concluding sentence that pulls all the main points together. Note the following example, from the précis paragraph at the top of this page:

The stakes are high: no academic skill will be more valuable to you than the ability to write clearly and effectively.

> ASSIGNMENT. During the next two weeks, write summary paragraphs of three passages: one from your history reading, one from your science text, and one from literature. If the passage is a difficult one for you, make it less than one chapter. The literature passage should be a complete unit of thought, possibly more or less than a chapter.

Throughout the school year (and beyond!) you should make a regular practice of summary writing, especially when confronted with difficult material. Schedule at least three of the following activities to do over the next two months.

> ASSIGNMENT. Write a summary of each chapter in a nonfiction book.

> ASSIGNMENT. Read and summarize in one paragraph a magazine article on a subject of interest to you.

> EXERCISE. Write a synopsis (a summary of a fictional plot) consisting of five sentences--no more, no less--of the plot of your favorite book or movie. Concentrate on the main action; don't get involved in subplots.

> ASSIGNMENT. Write a summary of the first ten years of your life. Include the highlights, but you should also come to some conclusion about what you learned and how you developed through these years.

> ASSIGNMENT. Summarize your favorite song. You may quote some of the key lines or phrases, but be sure to enclose them inside quotation marks.

BUSINESS REPORTS

It may surprise (and dismay) you that report writing doesn't end with school. In many branches of business and government, employees are often required to submit a proposal, research a market, or conduct a feasibility study on whether a project or direction would be worthwhile. All of these require research, organization, lots of thought, *and* a written report. Charts, graphs, tables, and pictures may be helpful too, but the heart of the study is the written report.

This composition must be logically thought-out and clearly expressed. Any employee who can do both the thinking and the expressing is well worth his hire. These skills are especially useful if you go into business for yourself, because your success will depend largely on how well you present your service or products.

In this section, you will do two **feasibility studies**. According to the Oxford American Dictionary, a feasibility study is "undertaken to decide whether a proposed course of action is suitable"--that is, sensible, or profitable, or wise, or the best of many options. A feasibility study lists all the applicable categories of a project and assigns time estimates and costs for each, concluding with an analysis and recommendation. When accomplished, a thorough and accurate study helps all the parties involved to make a decision.

The idea of a feasibility study shouldn't seem scary or foreign. You do many of them every day in your head. Think back to when you were about 12 years old, and your mother said, "Please go to the store and get some milk." Right away your mind would begin calculating the logistics--a mental "feasibility study" that might look like this:

MILK EXPEDITION PLAN

Where do I get the money?

Does Mom want a gallon or half-gallon?

What kind of milk--whole, 2% or chocolate?

When should I go? Now? I'm expecting a phone call. Should I ask Mom if it can wait an hour? (She'll probably say, "No, because you'll forget.") Can I get my little brother to do it? Probably not; Mom always vetoes suggestions like that.

How do I get there? Skateboard? Bicycle? Walk?

Could I do something I like on the way? Stop at Bret's? Buy an ice cream bar? (Should I ask Mom if I can spend the milk change?)

This could go on, but you probably get the idea.

A more complex proposition would require you to write down your questions and answers. Assume you want some extra money. You see a "Help Wanted " sign in the window of a local fast-food restaurant. Should you apply? A feasibility study might involve these considerations:

QUESTIONS	ACTION TO TAKE
A. What kind of work would I do?	a. Ask an employee.
B. Would I like it?	b. List your experiences, what you enjoy doing, your job skills, etc.
C. What does the restaurant pay?	c. Ask an employee or manager.
D. Is the pay acceptable?	d. Discuss with your parents.

(If it looks good so far, set up an interview time.)

E. What hours could I work?	e. Discuss with parents (school comes first).
F. How would I get to work and back? If by car, what is the cost?	f. Figure gas mileage, maintenance, etc.
G. How should I dress for the interview?	g. Ask parents, others.
H. What kind of clothes do I need for the work?	h. Ask restaurant manager during interview.
I. Would my attitude be right for this type of work?	i. Think over responsibilities carefully and evaluate your attitude to them.
J. What's my analysis and recommendation?	j. Think and write down your conclusions.

To conduct a feasibility study, follow these steps:

1. Write down all the questions you will need to answer.

2. Find the information that answers the questions (talk to people who know, look up reference sources in the library, go online, write letters, etc.).

3. Write a report that explains your findings. The report should follow this general outline:

    I. A statement of the problem or the situation you set out to address
    II. A summary of the options
    III. An explanation of the option you chose, and the reasons why you chose it, as well as a projection of the costs in time and money
    IV. A short concluding statement

Choose one project from each group below on which to conduct a study. The "A" project you choose should take no more than a week, but the "B" project will require more research and may stretch out over several weeks while you gather information. Perhaps you have an idea for a similar project. If so, feel free to tailor your own; just discuss it with your teacher or parent to clarify your goals and be sure that the project is worthwhile.

GROUP A	GROUP B
1. Should I go to college?	1. What could be our most enjoyable and cost-effective vacation this year?
2. If so, how will I pay for it?	
3. How should I change my diet?	2. How can I reach my goal of becoming a _____?
4. What are my best times for study and work?	
5. What are the most worthwhile books for the purpose of ____?	3. What is the best use for the vacant lot nearby?
	4. If I could visit any place in the world when I'm 21, where would it be?

PART TWO: LANGUAGE POWER

An experienced writer is like an animal trainer who has taught his tigers to go through rings of fire and snarl on command. Language itself is like a "wild animal" that must be trained--it's huge, sprawling, and difficult to handle at times. Even worse, perhaps, are the times it's flat and passive and won't do anything for you except roll over and play dead. Knowing the nature of the beast (that is, how language works) and the tricks to make it perform are important to developing confidence in writing. Part Two will help you better understand language.

This section is arranged a little differently from the rest of the book, in that you will be doing exercises rather than assignments. These exercises will teach you some tricks of the language trade and give you a chance to recognize and practice them.

The exercises are set off in boxes, as they were in the previous section, but some of them are very short. A suggested plan for working through this section in seven weeks is outlined below: you may use it as is or adapt it to your own schedule. Page numbers indicate the pages you are to study or review.

WEEK ONE
1. Ex. A-l, A-2, A-3 (pp. 30-32)
2. Ex. A-4 (p. 33)
3. Ex. A-5 (p. 36)
4.   "   "

WEEK TWO
1. Ex. B-l, B-2 (pp. 37-38)
2. Ex. B-3, B-4 (p. 39)
3. Ex. B-5, B-6 (pp. 40-41)
4. Ex. B- 7, B-8 (pp. 42-43)

WEEK THREE
1. Finish B-8
2. Ex C-1 (pp 43-44)
3: "   "
4. Ex. C-2 (p. 44)

WEEK FOUR
1. Ex. C-3 (p. 47)

2. Ex. C-4 (p. 48)
3. Ex. C-5 (p. 48)

WEEK FIVE
1. Ex. C-6 (p. 49)
2. Ex. C-7 (p. 49)
3. Ex. C-8 (p. 49)
4. Ex. D-1 (p. 50)

WEEK SIX
1. Ex. D-2 (p. 50)
2. Ex. D-3 (p. 51)
3. Ex. D-3   "
4. Ex. D-4   "

WEEK SEVEN
1. Ex. D-5 (p. 51)
2. Ex. D-6   "
3. Ex. D-7   "
4. Ex. D-7   "

A. PARAGRAPHS

PARAGRAPH PRINCIPLES

Ever since you learned to read, you have understood what a paragraph looks like: a series of written lines following an indented first line. It takes longer to understand what a paragraph *is:* a group of sentences written around a single idea. That idea may or may not be clearly stated in the paragraph itself. But there must be a single idea, or the paragraph will lack unity. Unity is the first principle of a paragraph.

If the main idea is **explicit** (clearly stated), it will be expressed in a **topic sentence**. All the other sentences will provide details, examples, or other kinds of support, but the topic sentence is the "flag" that signals the central message. The topic sentence often occurs at the beginning of a paragraph, but the writer may wish to place it at the end, or even bury it in the middle. You may not consciously notice them, but topic sentences help direct your thinking to follow the author's lead.

> EXERCISE A-1. Read the following paragraphs and determine where the topic sentences occur. Copy them in your notebook, then check your resu1ts with the answers on page 101.

1. The Rhine is Europe's most picturesque and legendary river. These broad waters, guarded by medieval castles, have served as the setting for tales of Norsemen and Teutons, Vikings and barbarian kings. Gazing up at the surrounding cliffs, one can easily imagine Thor swinging his hammer or the Valkyrie sweeping down on their battle steeds. No wonder some have called it "the river of the gods."

2. By the end of the day, Trenton was firmly in the grasp of the Continental Army. All the Hessian troops had surrendered, Colonel Herkimer was under house arrest, and the captured Christmas dinner was safely quartered in American stomachs. The ragged Continentals, now sporting boots with soles and coats without patches, were bedded down for their first warm, comfortable night in weeks. But the true gains went far beyond creature comforts. In spite of the odds, Washington had pulled off a master stroke: seized the initiative, frightened the British high command, and saved his army. Trenton was the true turning point of the War for Independence.

3. It was a large lovely garden, with soft green grass. Here and there over the grass stood beautiful flowers like stars, and there were twelve peach-trees that in the springtime broke out into delicate blossoms of pink and pearl, and in the autumn bore rich fruit. The birds sat on the trees and sang so sweetly that the children used to stop their games in order to listen to them. "How happy we are here!" they cried to each other.

Oscar Wilde, *The Selfish Giant*

4. In such a country, you will perceive at once that it is impossible that there should be anything of what you call a "solid" kind; but I dare say you will suppose that we could at least distinguish by sight the Triangles, Squares, and other figures, moving about as I have described them. On the contrary, we could see nothing of the kind, not at least so as to distinguish one figure from another. Nothing was visible, nor could be visible, to us, except Straight Lines. The necessity of this I will speedily demonstrate.

Edwin A. Abbot, *Flatland*

5. When the people of America reflect that they are now called upon to decide a question, which in its consequences must prove one of the most important that ever engaged their attention, the propriety of their taking a very comprehensive, as well as a very serious, view of it will be evident.

John Jay, *The Federalist*

WORDSMITH CRAFTSMAN - PART TWO

6. There was a king with a large jaw and a queen with a plain face on the throne of England. There was a king with a large jaw and a queen with a fair face on the throne of France. In both countries it was clearer than crystal to the Lord of the State preserves of loaves and fishes that things in general were settled forever.

Charles Dickens,
A Tale of Two Cities

Not all paragraphs contain a topic sentence. If the unifying thought is clear, though not stated in a single sentence, we say it is **implicit**. Rather than a topic sentence, the paragraph rallies around a "topic idea." The following exercise will be a little more challenging for you, because you will have to express the topic idea of each paragraph in your own words.

> EXERCISE A-2. In your notebook, write a short statement of the topic idea in each of the following paragraphs. Compare your sentences with mine on p. 101.

1. It is 8:30 on a summer evening. In the west the sun is going down behind a pile of clouds. The shouts and laughter of children playing drifts my way as I sit on the porch swing with some neglected mending in my lap. The smell of cut grass fills the air. Memories of past summers emerge in my mind like the serene stars in the evening sky.

2. One dollar and eighty-seven cents. That was all. And sixty cents of it was in pennies. Pennies saved one and two at a time by bulldozing the grocer and the vegetable man and the butcher until one's cheeks burned with the silent imputation of parsimony that such close dealing implied. Three times Della counted it. One dollar and eighty-seven cents. And the next day would be Christmas.

O. Henry, *The Gift of the Magi*

3. Socrates looked at [the jailer] and said: "I return your good wishes, and will do as you bid." Then turning to us, he said, "How charming the man is; since I have been in prison he has always been coming to see me, and at times he would talk to me, and was as good as could be to me, and now see how generously he sorrows for me. But we must do as he says, Crito; let the cup be brought, if the poison is prepared: if not, let the attendant prepare some." Plato, *Paedo*

4. Woodrow Wilson High hulks like a pile of sullen brick in the center of town. Paint is chipping liberally from the plastered walls and every room sports at least one broken window that has never been repaired. Books are falling apart and classroom space is so scarce that some classes have to be held in hallways. Student attitude and discipline reflect the poor condition of the building. But WWH is not the only decrepit school in our city; it may not even be the worst.

5. The rafters of the steel building clang with the distinctive pitches of dozens of breeds: Pomeranians, Great Danes, Spaniels, Afghans, and a handful of new varieties we have never heard of. Anxious owners are grooming their pets and trying to communicate confidence. The judges stroll about with an air of busy preoccupation, careful not to show too much interest in any one dog.

6. Derek dropped silently to the ground behind the old shed and crouched beside the window. Gradually voices began to reach his ears. "No!" he heard Celia exclaim. "I'll never tell you where the treasure is buried!" Next moment, the sound of an evil laugh made Derek's flesh crawl.

You have read thousands, perhaps tens of thousands of paragraphs in your life. From each of them you have gathered some sense of unity without even thinking about it. The second principle of the paragraph, coherence, may be a bit more difficult to grasp. **Coherence** means that the sentences fit together into a logical whole. Each sentence is like one member of a relay team, who "hands off" the train of thought to the next sentence until the main point of the paragraph is completed. If any sentence appears to change direction or drop the thought, the paragraph will lack coherence.

A person who speaks incoherently would sound something like this: "Did I tell you what happened the last time we went to the fall craft festival? It was two years ago--I remember because Tyler's first baby teeth had just come in and he was *so* cute, except the first time he bit me I nearly jumped out of my skin I was so surprised. Well, that's when we still had our green Chevy, you know the one the door fell off of. We had to wire it back on so you couldn't get into the car from that side. I used to pretend it wasn't really our car. Anyway, when we got to the festival . . . ."

It's okay to ramble in casual conversation, but a writer must take care that all the sentences of a paragraph hang together. Does a sentence not seem to fit? Is the order of the sentences confusing? Does the paragraph address more than one point?

> EXERCISE A-3. Each of the paragraphs below lack unity, or coherence, or both. In your notebook, state the problem with each paragraph in one complete sentence. When you're finished, check your answers on page 101.

1. Charles Darwin made many valuable contributions to science, but some of his conclusions are questionable. His study of wildlife on Galapogos Island was a model of systematic detective work that set standards for future scientists. He discovered significant variations among the island finches that promised fascinating insights into the natural world. As a result of his investigations, the science of naturalism received a new lease on life.

2. Swooping down a snow-covered slope on skis is the most thrilling experience I can imagine. The cold nips my nose, the clean sparkling air streams past my face, and my heart jumps to my throat as I pick up speed. The possibility of a tumble is always balancing on a razor-thin edge as the skis graze a mogul or skid on a turn. At the bottom of the hill, a mug of hot chocolate is waiting in the lodge.

3. When I look at the *Mona Lisa,* I always want to ask, "Lady, what are you thinking about?" Leonardo completed this, the world's most famous portrait, almost 500 years ago. The closer I look, the more inscrutable her expression becomes. The corners of her mouth are a little blurred, making it hard to classify her smile. The outside corners of her eyes are also indefinite, increasing the sense of mystery in the overall expression.

4. "Unfair! Unfair!" shouted the strikers along the picket line. For the second time, General Motors had refused to renegotiate their contract. Some of the angry picketers had brought their families along to hold signs and chant slogans.   TV news cameras were everywhere, recording the action. The dispute between labor and management centered mainly around health care benefits.   Most observers agreed that both sides had a point, but which side was right?

5. As a tax-paying citizen, I believe that giving money to "artists" to create offensive art is wrong. These people should not use common money to mock common values. I also believe that television has become so bad no child should be allowed to watch it. Why have an open sewer running into your living room?

6. The "starting crouch" in tennis is designed to get the player in a position of response. Grasp the racket stem firmly but flexibly with your leading hand (left or right). Stand with your feet about shoulder-width apart and your knees slightly bent, so you'll be ready to move quickly.   Your standing posture must be flexible also--ready to spring in any direction. The face of the racket should rest lightly against the fingers of your other hand. Make sure your shoes are not too tightly laced to be comfortable. Above all, watch the ball!

PARAGRAPH TYPES

Paragraphs fall into four basic types: narrative, descriptive, expository, and persuasive.

Narrative. A narrative is a sequence of events. It may be a personal experience of your own, or of someone you know, or a historical or fictional event. The idea of time is important in a narrative paragraph: the incidents happen in a well-defined order and usually lead to some sort of resolution.

Descriptive. Real estate ads and FBI "Wanted" posters describe, but what distinguishes a descriptive paragraph is the writer's desire to communicate a particular emotion or point about the object of the description.

Expository. Expository writing communicates information about any topic. Since the main purpose is to inform the reader, the style should be straightforward and factual. Textbooks, encyclopedias and much of what is called "non-fiction" is expository.

Persuasive. These paragraphs are written to provoke a response from the reader about a particular issue--if not agreement, then at least further thought. Lurking behind every persuasive paragraph is the idea of "ought" or "should." This is the kind of writing we usually associate with the editorial page of the newspaper.

The overall character of any single paragraph will be toward **description, narration, exposition** or **persuasion.** Most of the paragraphs in this book (as in most instructional books) are expository, but at times veer into persuasive writing (such as on page 1, where I make the case for keeping notes).

> EXERCISE A-4. Find, label, and copy in your notebook two examples of the four paragraph types (eight paragraphs in all). As a general rule, look in textbooks and newspapers for expository, editorial pages and magazines for persuasive, fiction for narrative and descriptive. If you want to avoid some writer's cramp, you can photocopy your paragraphs and paste them in your notebook, scrapbook-style.

PARAGRAPH ORGANIZATION

A well-written paragraph needs more than one unifying idea and supporting ideas. A well-written paragraph should also display **organization.** As you gain experience, you will be able to write paragraphs without even thinking about the organization; your experienced mind will just naturally arrange your sentences in an appropriate order. What sorts of order are we talking about here? It depends largely on the type of paragraph.

1. **Chronology.** One of the simplest and most obvious organizational patterns is arranging the events in the order in which they occurred. Narrative paragraphs are usually organized this way, as in these examples:

I walked into first-hour biology class with a jaunty air. "Good morning, Mr. Cuisak," said my professor. "Is that your prospectus I see?" I nodded, savoring his surprise. Only when I slapped the folder on his desk did I realize it was my sister's science project on bunnies.

Yorimoto, having been defeated in a battle against Oba Kage-chika, was forced to retreat with six of his followers. They ran with all speed through a forest, and, finding a large hollow tree, crept inside it for shelter.

(Japanese Folk Tale)

2. **Locality** is the pattern that often governs descriptive writing. This kind of organization puts objects or people in position for the reader. A writer may describe objects from side to side or top to bottom. Notice how this description leads the reader's "eye":

Empty soda cans, candy wrappers and fast food sacks trailed across the floor and piled up around the sofa. Tangled blankets and a stained pillow suggested that someone had been camping out in the family room. The corner of a long afghan stretched across the floor like an arrow, pointing toward the open door to the patio. Was that where we would find our prey at last?

Another way of using locality is to begin with the general scene and gradually focus on one part of it, or to begin with a specific point and move out to take in the big picture. It's like a movie camera "zooming in" on a single object or person, or pulling away from a detail to include the entire scene.

General to specific:

A booming wind tunneled down the city street, whipping the flags on the International Mall into a wild dance. Looming towers of steel and glass dwarfed the scurrying pedestrians. On the corner of 47th and Elm, the huddled old woman rocked like a buoy on the ocean, one narrow foot timorously extended to the edge of the curb.

Specific to general:

The sinewy hands pounded the keyboard so forcefully that a glass of water, perched at the corner of the baby grand, vibrated in place. Groans escaped the pianist, as though squeezed out under the pressure of his artistic vision. But the music he was literally sweating out was merely background noise to the exuberant crowd at the Seven Palms Club.

The image of a movie camera zooming in and out can also be helpful when considering our next two organizational patterns: induction and deduction.

3. **Induction** begins with a specific example or illustration and uses it to support a general statement. In the first example below (an expository paragraph), the dramatic picture of an individual crisis is used to introduce the subject of cardiac arrest. In the second example (narrative), the focus on the smile of one little girl expands to include an entire room of happy Honduran children at Christmastime.

It may come in the night--a sudden, gripping pain that wakes you from a sound sleep and sends waves of panic through your brain. Your breath comes faster: *What's happening?* It strikes about 650,000 people each year in the U.S., most of them men over 60 years old. It's one of a number of conditions commonly called a "heart attack."

The thin face broke into a radiant smile as two grimy but eager hands reached up to take the brightly-wrapped package. *"Gracias!"* Maria's squeal of delight was echoed around the room from dozens of Honduran children as the presents under the tree found owners. Soon they were racing to and fro, displaying their new treasures to anyone who would look.

4. **Deduction** works in the opposite direction by beginning with a general statement and sharpening the focus to a single incident or detail. In the first paragraph below (expository), a panoramic picture of banks closing across the country comes to focus on a single bank in a small Texas town. The second example (a persuasive paragraph) begins with a summary of poor educational performance nationwide before getting "up close and personal" on a specific example of someone whose prospects are limited by his dismal education.

For the first few months after the market crash, an uneasy quiet settled over the nation. Investors reassured themselves that they were only going through a correction and would emerge bruised but not busted. Then, quietly, a few big-city banks closed. Then a few more. Then many more. The panic began as a whisper and grew to a roar. On May 9, 1930, it reached a sleepy little town in east Texas.

"The schools aren't doing their job." This is a favorite rant of TV pundits and politicians on both sides of the aisle. Newspapers are full of stories about ninth-graders who can't locate the USA on a map, high school students who can't figure percentages, graduates who are functionally illiterate. But what does a third-rate education mean in the real world, to someone from the *barrio*, like Henry Salazar?

5. **Definition** or **Classification** is often required in expository writing, but may be helpful in narrative or persuasive types as well. Aristotle's classic formula for definitions is still a good overall approach: begin by placing the term or word to be defined in an appropriate category, then fill in details or examples to show how it is different from other members of that category.

Fortitude is one of the four cardinal virtues. Together with prudence, temperance and justice, fortitude is recognized as a hallmark of a worthy man or woman. It is the ability to take the hard way, to stick to a difficult course, and to endure the opposition of others.

Primates are the highest class of mammals. In addition to standard mammalian traits, they exhibit the ability to walk upright, to use opposing thumbs, and to reason on a basic level. Some primates can even recognize simple words and their meanings.

6. **Comparison** is another useful pattern of organization for expository or persuasive paragraphs. Difficult or technical concepts can often be explained by showing their similarities to everyday situations.

The process by which glucose is converted to usable energy mostly takes place in the mitochondria of each individual cell. The mitochondria can be imagined as "power plants" for the production of ADT. Day and night, seven days a week, these microscopic "factories" are continually converting one form of energy to another.

I draw my idea of the form of government from a principle in nature, which no art can overturn: that the more simple anything is, the less liable it is to be disordered, and the easier repaired when disordered; and with this maxim in view, I offer a few remarks on the much boasted constitution of England.
Thomas Paine, *Common Sense*

7. **Exploration** can be an effective tool of the persuasive paragraph. Here the author takes the attitude of thinking through a problem. A series of questions and answers can provide a sound framework, as long as it doesn't go on too long and become repetitious.

Everybody seems to have his own definition of "art," but definitions may confuse more than they explain. Is art, as some say, "the true, the good and the beautiful"? The problem with that definition is, I've seen ugly pictures that were true. Is it merely "self-expression," as others insist? If so, the scribbles of a three-year-old would qualify. Is it a tool of social conscience? A tract would do the same job with a lot less fuss. So what is this thing we call art?

8. **Cause and Effect** is simply stating a fact and listing the consequences of it. It's common in expository and persuasive writing.

For want of a nail, the horse was lost. For want of a horse, the leader was lost. For want of a leader the charge was lost, and for want of a charge the battle was lost. For the loss of the battle a kingdom fell, and it all came about for want of a nail.

Anonymous

In every state of these oppressions we have petitioned for redress in the most humble terms. Our repeated petitions have been answered only by repeated injury. A prince whose character is thus marked by every act which may define a tyrant, is unfit to be the ruler of a free people.

The Declaration of Independence

EXERCISE A-5. In your notebook, write one original example of each pattern of organization (eight paragraphs in all). Use a combination of narrative, descriptive, expository, and persuasive paragraphs. Study the examples carefully and make sure you understand the organizational pattern before you begin writing.

B. WRITING TECHNIQUES THAT REALLY WORK!

Writing may not be your favorite thing to do. In fact, you may have convinced yourself that you can't do it at all. But it is possible to improve your writing, once you've learned some time-honored techniques. As in most skills, practice makes . . . not perfect, but much better.

USE MORE VERBS--AND BETTER ONES

Verbs give our language vigor and color, but many beginning writers (even some experienced ones) pay little attention to them. It's not hard to use verbs effectively; it's a matter of training yourself to *pay attention* when you write. Learn to recognize weak spots in your writing, and to determine when a little more attention should be paid to the verbs. Here are some examples of weak spots:

1. Replace dull, colorless verbs with more descriptive verbs.

> Kyla *sat* on the edge of her seat, ready to jump.
> Kyla *perched* on the edge of her seat, ready to jump.

> Lyndon Johnson *won* the election in 1964.
> Lyndon Johnson *swept* the election in 1964.

2. Replace some verb-adverb combinations with stronger verbs.

> People who *laugh loudly* at the serious parts annoy me.
> People who *guffaw* at the serious parts annoy me.

> The fans *moved quickly* past the turnstiles.
> The fans *poured* through the turnstiles.

3. Replace some linking verbs (such as *am, is, are, was, were,* etc.) with strong action verbs. Be sure the stronger verbs are accurate and truthful.

> Lisa *was angry* with the referee.
> Lisa *seethed* at the referee.

> The committee *was pleased* with the report and *was encouraging* about the
>   author's plan.
> The committee *cheered* the report and *encouraged* the author to pursue the plan.

> EXERCISE B-1. Rewrite the following sentences, paying special attention to the verbs. Check the rewrites on page 101 after writing yours. HINT: if you're stumped on some of these, try rearranging the nouns.

1. My brother was very happy with the gift.
2. Todd ran past the finish line.

3. One by one, guerrillas moved quietly by the guard post.
4. Rhoda was excited about going to Japan.
5. Algebra makes me mad.

LET'S GET PERSONAL

Humans respond instinctively to other humans--that's the way we are made. Effective writers strive for personal appeal in their work whenever appropriate, often by simply choosing a personal noun over an impersonal one.

The teaching community is facing a shortage of jobs today.
Teachers today are facing a shortage of jobs.

Stop that *car!*
Stop that *driver!*

The media thinks it can control our minds.
Some journalists think they can control our minds.
(Notice the qualifier "some"--we can't assume that *all* of any group thinks anything.)

> EXERCISE B-2. Rewrite the following sentences to make them more personal. Compare your answers with those on page 101.

1. The low-income community feels neglected by government.
2. How large is the science department at that school?
3. The clothing industry wants higher tariffs.
4. Congress has become detached and corrupt.
5. The class of 2004 looks forward to the future with anticipation.

NOTE: While making an effort to be more personal, try not to overuse the words "people" or "person" too much. If possible, substitute a word with a more concrete definition.

People in this country live in a hurry-up society.
Americans live in a hurry-up society.

Give your check to the *person* at the window.
Give your check to the *cashier* at the window.

BE SPECIFIC (AND AGAIN I SAY, BE SPECIFIC!)

General sentences may seem acceptable for general information: "Our situation was desperate." "It was a good year." But even when summarizing, competent writers make the effort to be as specific as possible: "We were pressed against the river bank with no avenue of retreat." "It was a productive year for melon farmers." *Say what you mean.* In most cases, this means being specific.

Ballooning is fun.
Hot-air ballooning is soothing and exhilarating at the same time.

There is a sense of good racial relationships in the neighborhood.
The interaction between black and white neighbors seems relaxed and cordial.

> EXERCISE B-3. Rewrite these sentences to be more specific. You'll find you can be very creative. Each example on pp. 101-102 is just one of many possibilities.

1. That was the scariest movie I ever saw.
   (Hint: try focusing on the scariest *part* of the movie.)
2. People were standing around sadly.
3. I learned a lot my junior year.
4. That car is not safe.
5. We look forward to the future with hope.

PREFER ACTIVE VOICE OVER PASSIVE

"Voice" refers to the relationship between the subject of the sentence and the verb. The "active over passive" rule is well known, yet even professional writers fall into the passive habit. In **active** sentences the subject is doing the action:

<small>subject</small>
Mrs. Bates handed out our assignments.

In **passive** sentences the subject is receiving the action:
<small>subject</small>
Our assignments were handed out by Mrs. Bates.

Active voice is direct and forceful. **Passive** voice is meandering and inert. In some cases passive voice is better, such as when the person (or thing) "doing the action" is unknown or not as important as the object: "The library had been decorated for a party." But active sentences make for stronger writing.

> EXERCISE B-4. Rewrite the following sentences in active voice. This time, there is only one right answer (except that you will have to choose your own subject for #3). Check answers on page 102.

1. The fans were thrilled with Saturday's game.
2. Basic food supplies were desperately needed by the Rwandans.
3. Your prompt attention is appreciated.
4. The statue had been broken by thugs.
5. The building was repaired by volunteers from the U. S.

SHOW, DON'T TELL!

This rule is related to being specific. A writer has the opportunity not merely to describe but also to create pictures with words. How is this done? The same way a painter paints: by stroking in lines, colors, light and shades to coordinate into one whole. A writer's "brushstrokes" are the details that he or she uses to highlight an emotion, action, or mood.

He looks happy and pleased.
He laughs as he opens the present, shouting, "Thanks, Grandma! It's just what I
    wanted!"   (Notice how the quote communicates the speaker's mood.)

The room was very messy.
Food wrappers, empty soda cans and crumpled papers littered the floor.

> EXERCISE B-5. The following sentences merely *tell* Rewrite each of them to *show*. Use at least one direct quotation in this exercise. Compare your sentences with the rewrites on page 102.

1. I could tell she was very disappointed.
2. Mom looked uncomfortable.
3. The army was disorganized.
4. The audience was bored.
5. The children seemed very excited.

CUT THE VERBIAGE

Don't confuse "verbiage" with "foliage." The latter is a cluster of leaves; the former is a cluster of words--too many words. Beginning writers should always strive for three goals:

    1. **aptness** (the right word or phrase for the author's meaning)
    2. **simplicity** (the plainest terms possible for explaining a concept)
    3. **clarity** (words chosen and arranged specifically to get the message across)

Doesn't it seem obvious that these are the keys to good communication? And yet much of today's professional writing (produced by university professors, lawyers and government agents) is almost unreadable. Here's an example taken from a toothpaste tube:

[This toothpaste] has been shown to be an effective decay-preventive
dentifrice that can be of significant value when used in a conscientiously
applied program of oral hygiene and regular professional care.

In plain English, this simply means that the toothpaste will help keep your teeth healthy if you brush daily and see a dentist once in a while. The sentence is an illustration of what happens when committees do the writing.

For beginning writers, important-sounding words may not be the problem so much as mindlessly repeating the "padded" phrases they hear over the air, in speeches, and in ordinary conversation. Notice how clumsy these phrases sound, compared to their one-word counterparts.

Moral judgments are more confusing in this day and age.
Moral judgments are more confusing today.

You should work out on a daily basis to maintain health.
You should work out daily to maintain health.

Unnecessary qualifiers can also "pad" your writing. Some qualifiers *are* necessary to specify the meaning. In an example on page 38 ("Some journalists think they can control our minds."), the qualifier "some" makes it clear that we are not accusing *all* journalists. But qualifiers shouldn't become such a habit that they pop up in every other sentence. Notice how they detract from the force of the sentences below:

Interrupting is sort of a pet peeve of mine.
Interrupting is my pet peeve. (or, one of my pet peeves)

Some if not all college graduates earn higher incomes.
Most college graduates earn higher incomes.

Good writing is concise; every word counts. Loading up your sentences with "big words," padded phrases or unneeded qualifiers will lose a reader's interest and indicate that you may not have that much to say.

> EXERCISE B-6. Rewrite these sentences to eliminate the unnecessary verbiage. Check your rewritten sentences with those on page 102.

1. Treating customers in a rude manner is the surest way to terminate your job experience.
2. Owing to the fact that the temperature was below zero, the men were in serious danger of hypothermia.
3. She is a woman who knows her mind.
4. In the event of combustibles igniting in the cooking quarters, patrons will be evacuated in a hasty but orderly manner through the hotel lobby.
5. In this day and age, men and women face a variety of stresses and tensions, metaphorically speaking.

AVOID CLICHES (LIKE THE PLAGUE)

You know what I mean--those tried-and-true analogies that no longer ring true. After all, what does "work like a dog" mean? Most dogs don't do that much work. Other similes and metaphors are fine for speech but should be avoided in writing: "hard as a rock," "light as a feather," "going the whole nine yards," and "the whole enchilada." It takes thought, but thinking and writing go hand-in-hand. (Ooops--there's another cliché.)

EXERCISE B-7. Complete the similes below, substituting a new comparison for the one that will come immediately to mind. (Your new comparison should still make sense, however.)

Tough as _____   Neat as _____

Heavy as _____   Bold as _____

Firm as _____   Sick as _____

Bright as _____   Cold as _____

The brilliant writer George Orwell, in a 1946 essay titled "Politics and the English Language," agreed with me about clear and forceful English!   He concluded the essay with these rules:

1. Never use a metaphor, simile, or other figure of speech which you are used to seeing in print.
2. Never use a long word where a short one will do.
3. If it is possible to cut a word out, always cut it out.
4. Never use the passive where you can use the active.
5. Never use a foreign phrase, a scientific word, or a jargon word if you can think of an everyday English equivalent.

EXERCISE B-8. The three paragraphs below suffer from a number of ailments: weak sentences, vague or general terms, unnecessary words or phrases, etc. Review the problems and remedies we've discussed so far (pp. 37-42), and perform "surgery" on each paragraph to make it more specific, forceful and interesting. Do your best with each of these, then check the rewrites on page 102.

---

1. After twelve long weeks, the EMT final exam was finally passed. No more long nights of staying up until 1:00 a.m. studying. No more struggling through afternoon classes feeling like death warmed over. In the long run, Fred had to kind of admit it was probably worth it, but it was an experience he really never wanted to go through again.

2. Lewis Griffin was a veteran of 300 jumps. He knew what he was doing when it came to diving out of aircraft. So it was with total confidence that he made a routine jump out of a plane 13,000 feet over central Iowa. In an unexpected development, however, another diver crashed into him accidentally and knocked him unconscious. Suddenly Lew was dropping like a stone, arms flapping like a rag doll, unable to help himself.

3. Every night, thousands of homeless men and women are sleeping in America's streets and alleys. The homeless community has been neglected by the American system. The fact that these people have no homes should be troublesome to the vast majority of their fellow citizens. Can or should anything be done?

C. STEPS TOWARD A PERSONAL WRITING STYLE

Remember the comparison of language to a wild animal on page 29? To "tame" language, you must think about it. Considering various ways to make a point, choosing and discarding words, and deciding against one type of sentence in favor of another are ways a writer develops a personal *style*. You've probably noticed differences in the way various authors write. Those differences make up each individual style.

We're moving out of the territory of right and wrong. Forging a personal style involves making choices among options that may all be correct. The choice you make depends on your assessment of what's most effective at any given point.

EMPHASIS

Unless it's very badly done, every piece of writing has at least one main point. **Emphasis** is a way of drawing "arrows" to the places where a reader should pay particular attention. Certain phrases make this obvious, such as, "to summarize," or "the most important thing to remember is . . ." Textual devices like bold print or italics can also stress the point. But writers who don't want to sound like a textbook must develop more subtle ways to emphasize.

1. **Word order**. The climax of a story occurs near the end. In the same way, the position of greatest emphasis in a sentence or paragraph is at the end. Notice the subtle change in emphasis in these two sentences:

> An ancient oak tree stood in the center of town.
> In the center of town stood an ancient oak tree.

The tree is the subject of both sentences, and subjects are usually placed at the beginning. But if the oak tree has particular significance in what follows, a writer may wish to hint at that significance with unusual word order. Here's another example that everyone should recognize.

> The question is whether to be or not to be.
> To be or not to be, that is the question.

Most of us will agree that the second version sounds better, but is that only because we are used to it? Shakespeare may have considered both versions, but decided on the latter because of its subtle emphasis on the last word. Throughout the play, the speaker of these famous lines wavers between certainty and doubt about what he should do-- uncertainty is the point, emphasized by placing the word "question" at the end of the line.

2. **Long/short contrast.** A good writer tries to employ a variety of sentence lengths: some very long, some shorter, some joined together with connecting words, some broken up with colons and semi-colons. In general, most of your sentences should be of medium length or longer; very short sentences can be reserved for emphasis.

> For fifteen years Europe shook, bled, and trembled under the fateful tread of one man. That man was Napoleon.
> The day was bright and sunny, I felt loved and appreciated and I hadn't fouled up once. Then I got out of bed.

Short sentences deliver a punch, but too many of them can pound a reader until they all sound alike. Some well-known authors have built a style around "punchy" sentences, but most of us should reserve them for emphasis.

The same rule applies for short paragraphs, as in this example:

> When the security guard hesitated, then motioned to him, Benny could have laughed with relief. Mishaps had plagued him all the way to the concert, and he had arrived too late to be admitted with the press corps. He stood at the barricades surrounded by screaming teenagers, pouring out his sob story to the officer and praying that the man would take pity. At the much-desired signal, his heart leapt; high time for his luck to change.
> That's what he thought--but he was wrong.

> EXERCISE C-I. Find and copy in your notebook five examples of words arranged for emphasis. Speeches and "notable" quotes are likely places to find these (check *Readers' Digest* or *Bartlett's Familiar Quotations*). Then find and copy three examples (one paragraph each) of short sentence contrast.

3. **Parallel construction and repetition.** By now you should know that all English sentences are constructed according to pattern. Although our language allows great variety, the rules stay the same: subjects tell what the sentence is about, verbs tell what the subject is or does, adjectives always modify nouns, etc. The **construction** of a sentence is the pattern that it follows. The following two sentences have nothing in common but their construction, as the diagram shows.

Because she failed the first test, Jane dropped out.

Although our language allows great variety, the rules stay the same.

Parallel constructions are sentences or sentence parts that are arranged in a similar pattern. Here's a well-known example:

> "It is a far, far better thing that I do, than I have ever done; it is a far, far better rest that I go to than I have ever known."
>
> Charles Dickens, *A Tale of Two Cities*

The parallels here are obvious: "It is," followed by the repetition of the adverb ("far, far") modifying "better," then the introduction of a relative clause ("that I do/go to") contrasted with another relative clause ("than I have ever done," "than I have ever known"). Notice that the words are very simple; Dickens relies entirely on parallel construction for the impact of this sentence. Like other methods of emphasis, however, this one should be used carefully; save it for final paragraphs or main points.

Repetition is using the same word or phrase several times in a paragraph or longer passage. You have been taught to write sentences of varied lengths, use a variety of words and avoid repeating yourself. But a skillful writer understands when repetition is just the tool for making a point. Consider this paragraph from a speech by Theodore Roosevelt in 1899, when he was Governor of New York:

> Let us therefore boldly face the life of strife, resolute to do our duty well and manfully; resolute to uphold righteousness by deed and word; resolute to be both honest and brave, to serve high ideals with practical methods.
>
> "The Strenuous Life"

Not even an English teacher would be tempted to pick up a red pencil and strike out all those extra "resolutes." That's because it should be obvious to anyone that the repetition is *deliberate*. The word punctuates the beginning of each clause with the effect of a fist slamming a podium. With every "resolute," Governor Roosevelt hammers home his theme of "The Strenuous Life" of public service in a way no listener could miss. Careful use of repetition creates an echo in the reader's mind.

> EXERCISE C-2. Rewrite these famous examples of repetition and parallel construction so that they *don't* repeat. Try breaking one sentence into two, combining short sentences, or rearranging sentence parts. Then compare your version with the original quotation.

1. If nominated, I will not run; if elected, I will not serve.
   Lyndon Johnson, 1968

2. We shall pay any price, bear any burden, meet any hardship, support any friend, oppose any foe to assure the survival and the success of liberty.
   John F. Kennedy

3. We shall fight on the beaches, we shall fight on the landing grounds, we shall fight in the fields and in the streets, we shall fight in the hills; we shall never surrender. . .
   Winston Churchill

4. This royal throne of kings, this sceptered isle,
   This earth of majesty, this seat of Mars,
   This other Eden, demi-paradise,
   This fortress built by nature for herself
   Against infection and the hand of war;
   This happy breed of men, this little world . . .
   This blessed plot, this earth, this realm, this England . . .
   Shakespeare, Richard II, Act 2, Scene 1

MAKING TRANSITIONS

Transitions are words or phrases that form bridges between one thought and the next. Below are some of the most familiar transitional words and phrases:

likewise often in addition	These underline or provide further support for a point already made.
chiefly even more mostly	These emphasize an important point.
but on the other hand admittedly nevertheless	These signal a contrasting or opposing point.
for instance such as like	These introduce an example or illustration.
therefore as a result thus	These indicate a consequence flowing from what was said earlier.
in effect in other words that is	These indicate a restatement of the point just made.
close by there further back in the distance	These indicate place.
as soon as later next at last	These indicate time.

in conclusion   These signal you to get your coat and hat: it's almost over!
finally
to sum up

Neglecting transitions is a common mistake of beginning writers. They know where they're headed (or at least think they know) and aim straight for it. But quick jumps from one point to another can be confusing for the reader, simply because we don't all think alike. A connection that's obvious to you may not be so obvious to me. Transitional words and phrases serve as "road signs" or markers to indicate the direction your thoughts are taking, so the reader can follow more easily.

Transitions are especially important in expository and persuasive paragraphs, where the *sequence* of thought may be as important as the thoughts themselves. Sometimes, in order to understand *d;* I must know *a* and *b,* and how they prove *c.* Transitional phrases can help keep the sequence in mind or make it clearer.

> EXERCISE C-3. Find an article 4-10 paragraphs long in a newspaper or magazine. Read the article through so you understand the drift. Then, in your notebook, copy each topic sentence or topic idea in sequence, as though they were the sentences of one double-spaced paragraph. Study the resulting paragraph, then add transitional words, phrases or sentences that will help the reader follow the story. See the example below for ideas on how this can be done. The abstract summary on pages 24-25 is another example.

In the second of these "before" and "after" paragraphs, the words in italics indicate the transitional phrases and sentences that were added.

Angela's story is one of grit and determination. Education was the way out. Angela did well there and was encouraged to aim higher. The state of Illinois offered her a scholarship in return for working three years in a needy community after her residency. For a while, in medical school, Angela's determination faltered. At age 41, the former welfare mother and resident of Chicago's public housing had become a pediatrician. "Now," says 21 year-old Joseph, "I'm real glad she did it." Dr. Blythe is clear about where she wants to practice medicine: "In a poor neighborhood."

Angela's story is one of grit and determination. *After her life had come to a dead end, Angela Blythe realized that* education was the way out. *Because she did so well in nursing school,* Angela was encouraged to aim higher. *Once she had received her advanced degree in biology,* the state of Illinois offered her a scholarship in return for working three years in a needy community after her residency. For a while, in medical school, Angela's determination faltered, *and so did her children's. But finally,* at age 41, the former welfare mother and resident of Chicago's public housing had become a pediatrician. "Now," says *her* 21-year-old *son* Joseph, "I'm real glad she did it." *In contrast to most med school graduates,* Dr. Blythe is clear about where she wants to practice: "In a poor neighborhood."

EXERCISE C-4. Follow the same procedure with another news article, then with an editorial or opinion piece. Which type of writing requires more transitions?

EXERCISE C-5. Find a news article 4-10 paragraphs long, but don't read it through. On scratch paper, copy any seven sentences from the article, selecting at random. List the sentences on separate lines; don't write them in paragraph form. Now cut the sentences apart so that you have seven strips. Read the article (finally!) and then see if you can arrange the sentences in a logical order that at least reflects the meaning. Now, copy the sentences in paragraph form in your notebook, adding transitions as needed to create a flow from one thought to another. You may need to add a sentence here and there to fill in gaps. With the help of transitions, you should end up with a paragraph that at least makes sense, even if it seems a little unbalanced.

"LOADED" WORDS AND SELECTIVE DETAIL

News reporters are supposed to be objective--they are simply to state the facts with no personal opinions mixed in. Even so, you may have read a few "news" articles that left you with the unmistakable impression that the writer fell on one side or the other of an issue. Of course, there was no clear statement of opinion--this was a news article, after all. So how did you receive your impression? Two ways: 1) certain words chosen for their effect, and 2) the details included by the writer.

The dictionary meaning of a word is called its **denotation.** But many words in common usage carry shades of meaning beyond the bare definition. These shades of meaning are known as **connotations.** Every word has at least one denotation, but not all have connotation. Those that do are "loaded words"--undercover words that can be used to draw subtle distinctions the reader may not even recognize.

Compare these sentences:

Sheila was *disabled* at age 13.
Sheila was *crippled* at age 13.

The second sentence has a greater impact, but you may not be sure why. Both the italicized words mean essentially the same thing, but "disabled" is rather bland, or neutral-- it arouses no strong feelings. "Crippled," on the other hand, is harsh, even cruel. Its **connotation** is negative, and it is more likely to provoke a negative response in the reader.

Here's a very short list of paired words with positive and negative connotations:

melancholy - gloomy
influence - brainwash
statesman - politician
tincture - taint
tactful - mealy-mouthed
complimentary - smarmy
dignified - stuffy

temperate - abstemious
faith - gullibility
thrifty - cheap
delicate - feeble
weep - blubber
inquisitive - nosy
clever - conniving

Choosing words with definite connotation is one way a writer can create a positive or negative impression. The second way is by highlighting certain details. Compare these two descriptions of a political figure:

A. This man is tall and well-built. His healthy complexion glows. Laugh lines surround his eyes and his smile comes often and easily. Speaking in a soft southern drawl, he leans forward, making me think he really cares about my opinion.

B. This man is tall, but stooped a little at the shoulders. His nose is bulbous and his florid face is puffy. His cornpone accent seems to clash with his small, shifty eyes. I hear the touch of a whine in his voice as he tells me what's wrong with this country.

Gentleman A appears warm, friendly and sympathetic. Gentleman B seems sneaky and conniving. Would it surprise you to learn that both descriptions apply to the same man? Both are accurate as far as the dictionary meanings (the denotations) of all the words are concerned. But by focusing on certain features, and describing those features in words with a particular connotation, a writer can create a strong impression without making *any* definite statements.

Let's take another look at how this is done. The following two paragraphs describe the same street in a New York City ghetto around 1900. In the first description we see a depressing place, in the second a poor but homelike community.

Hester Street was crowded with grimy tenements and overhead telegraph cables that angrily crossed out the sky. Overworked housewives shrilled at each other and at their children, a rag-tag mob playing violent games in the street. Decrepit old men filled up their pointless days in the stairwells, sharing worn-out memories.

Hester Street was crowded with grimy tenements and brimming with life. On any sunny day, strings of laundry fluttered like flags. Busy mothers called to each other across the pavement, mutually managing their rough-and-tumble children who never lacked for playmates. The "grandfather contingent" gathered in the stairwells and swapped tales that never grew old.

EXERCISE C-6. Paging through a thesaurus, you should be able to find many examples of positive-negative connotations. (For example, under "excuse (v)" you will find "forgive" and "indulge.") In your notebook, make a list of at least 20 paired words, similar to the list on p. 48.

EXERCISE C- 7. Choose a public figure who appears often in the news and write contrasting descriptions of him or her. For the positive side, focus on the details of that person's face, posture, or voice that are especially attractive, and describe them in words of positive connotation (consult your thesaurus again). For the negative description, locate the less flattering features and words.

EXERCISE C-8. Now describe a place in a positive and a negative light. Choose a place you know, or study a picture from a magazine. What words and details will create an image of comfort or of despair? Is the living room orderly and neat, or stiff and oppressive? Is the street homey and relaxed, or shabby and cluttered? What details support each view?

THE IMPORTANCE OF BEING HONEST

Remember George Orwell's rules on page 42? Actually, the list is not complete. He added one more:

6. Break any of these rules sooner than say anything outright barbarous.

Language is powerful: wars have begun, kingdoms have fallen and generations inspired by carefully planned and well-chosen words. Because of this power, a writer must use language responsibly, no matter what his motivation. Using words to persuade or move a reader, create a mood or capture attention is justified. Using words to deceive, mislead or shade the truth is never justified.

D. PRACTICE AND REVIEW EXERCISES

> EXERCISE D-1. Rewrite paragraphs 4,5, and 6 on page 32 to make them more coherent.

> EXERCISE D-2. The three paragraphs below are general, unfocused, and wordy. Rewrite them with a clear focus: add concrete details, comparison, or examples. Your paragraphs will be longer, but they should also be much more interesting.

1. Those who claim they just can't get ahead in life may need to examine their attitude and lifestyle, rather than their circumstances or lot in life. Often what's usually needed most is a willingness to take chances, to go out on a limb, to work hard. This country was built by people who did just that.

2. Many young people seem to think that friendship is merely liking someone enough to hang out with them. When they like the person, they are friends. When they stop, they are no longer friends. Most true friends like each other, of course, but real friendship goes deeper than that. Real friendship is probably quite rare.

3. I think we sometimes are too quick to judge someone else's motives. How do we know what another person is feeling or experiencing? Can we "walk a mile in their shoes"? Can we enter their lives and see through their eyes? Before we make up our minds about why someone did what they did, let's try to sympathize first.

EXERCISE D-3. This exercise will take a little imagination. Write an expository paragraph on the subject of "nilloes." You don't know what a nillo is? Neither do I! You determine what they are, and write an informative paragraph about some aspect of their existence (remember to be specific and keep your focus; don't try to explain everything about them). When that project is completed, write a persuasive paragraph on the same subject. A persuasive paragraph introduces the idea of "ought" or "should." Your persuasive paragraph about nillos must assume a situation that demands a solution.

EXERCISE D-4. Write two expository paragraphs about events in the news. You should know enough about each event to include specific facts. Write a topic sentence first, and make sure each sentence in the paragraph relates to it.

EXERCISE D-5. Rewrite the two paragraphs from D-4 for the average third- or fourth- grade reader. Think carefully about the words you use, add further explanation, and include an example, if possible.

EXERCISE D-6. Rewrite the two paragraphs from D-4 as persuasive paragraphs. Rewrite the topic sentence first, so that it states an opinion about the way things *ought* to be.

EXERCISE D- 7. By this time, you should have the original drafts of several letters in your notebook: letters of complaint, apology, support, request, etc. Choose three of them to rewrite. Make some sentences more specific, add a short contrasting sentence for emphasis, change a passive sentence to active, or otherwise improve the composition of the letter.

PART THREE: THE ESSAY

No student can escape THE ESSAY. Essays are everywhere: on tests, in the newspaper, in fat leather-bound volumes of "Collected Works," in literature textbooks and magazines of every sort. High school and college students are continually asked to read, analyze, and eventually write them. What's the big deal about essays?

An essay is the written expression of the author's thoughts, conclusions, or findings on any given subject. If that seems too broad a definition, let's take a moment to consider what the essay is *not*.

* It's not fiction because an essay is based on the thoughts, experiences, and sensations of an actual person in the actual world.

* It's not poetry because the ideas are not arranged in poetical form and do not rely on "poetical" language or imagery for their impact.

* It's not a simple narrative because the ideas are structured around a form other than mere sequence.

* It's not a news article or report because the overall tone is more personal.

* It's not a recipe, caption, resume, or instruction sheet, because at first glance it appears to have no practical application!

But even with all these exclusions, essays can be about anything and run in length from a few paragraphs to many pages (John Locke's *Essay on Human Understanding* covers two *volumes!).* The essay is excellent practice for all types of writing and a great exercise for planning, organizing, and thinking.

Essay writing is more than a school exercise, however. Any written expression of your thoughts that is centered on a single theme or idea can be considered an essay. Throughout your life, just such a written expression may be exactly what's required to get you into the college of your choice, secure the job of your dreams, remove an obstacle from your path, or change someone's mind about an important issue. In Part Three of this book, you will learn how to put together a well-written essay.

Are you excited yet? Let's get started.

ESSAY STRUCTURE

Every piece of writing must have some structure or form in order to make sense. Picking your way through an unstructured page is almost as difficult as finding a word in a dictionary that's not arranged in alphabetical order. Neither would have much reason for existing. Fortunately, the basic essay form is so simple you can memorize it right now. Here it is:

Introduction
Body
Conclusion

Think of it as a parade. First come the veterans with flags, the police car, or the high-stepping majorettes with a banner--any or all of which will clear the street and capture the attention of the crowd. The body of the parade can be two miles or two blocks long, and varied in color and pitch, but all of it moves in the same direction. Finally, a good parade should wind up with a designated conclusion--like a cleanup squad with "pooper-scoopers." After they go by the crowd spills into the street, understanding that the event is over and they will not be run over by a renegade float.

Within this basic outline of Introduction, Body, and Conclusion, almost all essays can be classified according to four familiar types: descriptive, narrative, expository, and persuasive. To these I will add one more: critical.

Although you have learned to identify individual paragraphs as descriptive, narrative, expository and persuasive, classifying an essay is not always simple. Most essays contain a *mixture* of narration, description, exposition, or persuasion--or all four. But only one type will characterize the overall essay, and with a little practice you should be able to classify a piece according to the dominant type.

> EXERCISE. Many of the articles in general interest magazines (such as *Readers Digest, The Saturday Evening Post, World & I,* or *Atlantic Monthly*) might be considered essays. Page through an issue of one of these magazines and find five short articles (two pages or less). Mark each paragraph with a "D," "N," "E," or "P" according to type (see p. 33 for definitions). Some may be difficult to classify-- take your best guess! Then determine the type of the entire essay.

WHERE DO IDEAS COME FROM?

Many students believe that writing is hard for them because they have nothing to write about. It may surprise you to learn that the very opposite is true--the problem is not that you have too little to write about, but that you have too much!

Think about it. After living through your childhood, you have become proficient in *all* the basic skills necessary for a successful life: walking, talking, reading, writing, arithmetic, and much more. You have had literally thousands of experiences--exciting, depressing, joyful, educational--you name it. You have formed numerous relationships with other people, and learned quite a bit about human behavior. If there's something you don't know, you probably have a good idea how to find out or whom to ask. You've seen, heard, felt, tasted, and smelled sensations that will stay with you for the rest of your life.

But when you are told to sit down and write, you may find that the words don't come. Worse, the ideas don't come. Write? About what? That blank piece of paper staring up at you looks as empty as your mind feels.

But your mind is not empty; just the opposite. It's crammed so full of thoughts, memories, ideas and experiences that you can't tell where one begins and another leaves off. It *looks* like a blank wall, but actually it's a treasury of material, packed very tightly. Your job is not to conjure subject matter out of the air, but to shake loose the material that's already in your head.

I won't pretend it's easy. But it *can* be done, if you are patient and painstaking and willing to practice. Anyone can learn to write an essay; the secret is to break the process into steps, and to concentrate on one step at a time.

THE TOPIC

The first step is determining what to write about. If you are told to write an essay on "love" or "friendship," don't try to start on an introductory paragraph right away. You don't yet know what to write about. What you have is only a **subject**: a general idea which could lead you in dozens of directions. Your first step, given a subject, is to narrow it down to a **topic**. The topic is what you will write about.

One technique for narrowing the subject is called clustering. Clustering is not the only way, but it's worth practicing because it can give you a visual picture of your thoughts. Here's how it works:

Find the word PEACE in the diagram below. This is the subject, and like most subjects it's very broad. Further thoughts about "peace" could lead to some very different topics. The point in clustering is to write down *every* word or phrase related to peace that comes to mind, and form connections between them.

My first thought is about inner peace and how that might be achieved. But what about in the rest of the world? Is peace even possible? When we look around us and listen to the news, the outlook for worldwide peace seems discouraging. But what about peace in my own family or within my circle of acquaintances? That might be within reach because much of it depends on me. If I am at peace within, I am more likely to be a peacemaker with those around me. And what feelings are created in me by the thought of peace? If it were a color, it would be as blue as the sky on a cloud-spotted, warm spring day.

54

After only a few minutes, I've come up with a map of my current thoughts on the subject of peace. Any of the "destinations" on this map would make an acceptable topic, but some are better than others. The most important rule for choosing a topic is, *make it specific.* The farther away you can get from the center of the diagram, the better your essay is likely to be. In practical terms, you'll find your best topics by exploring the outer branches of the cluster.

Thinking further about the idea of peace in the family, I might decide to concentrate on common courtesy as a way to maintain it. Of course there are other ways to this goal, and being at peace with myself will help me be courteous with others, but I must stay focused. The next step will provide a tool to keep this focus.

THE THESIS STATEMENT

A thesis statement is a clear, concise expression of the main point of the essay. It could actually appear in the text, but not necessarily--that's your decision. A thesis statement takes thought, but once you've written it, your focus is established.

Here are two possible thesis statements for my essay on peace in the family:

```
1. Those little acts of courtesy, even though they seem
   insignificant, can be the "oil" that helps a family
   operate smoothly.
2. Sometimes I don't feel like answering politely, but our
   family life has been much more peaceful since I started
   making the effort.
```

Each of these sentences will lead in slightly different directions. An essay built on the first sentence will concentrate on the idea that little things make a big difference. The second thesis statement is a variation on that theme: my personal responsibility to act courteously even when I don't feel like it..

If the topic of "peace in the family" doesn't appeal to you, notice how other branches in the cluster could be developed.

Topic: Peace in the Middle East
Thesis Statement: The centuries-old conflicts in the Middle East go so deep that any "peace" will probably be temporary.

Topic: Peace among friends
Thesis Statement: Even the closest friendships hit some rough spots, so I've learned to be prepared for hurt feelings and misunderstandings.

Topic: The color of peace
Thesis Statement: The deep unchanging color of the sky that day reflected the new sense of serenity that I had discovered.

> EXERCISE. Choose three of the general subjects listed below. Cluster first, then select a topic and write a thesis sentence on each of the subjects.

food	health	childhood
adventure	responsibility	friendship
education	war	work

Before moving on to writing essays, let's take one apart to see how it works.

> EXERCISE. Study the essay below, then follow the directions. Check your answers on page 102.

1. Determine the type (N, D, E, or P) of each paragraph, then classify the essay as a whole.
2. Write the thesis sentence.
3. Write a one-paragraph summary of the entire essay.
4. List three ways that the author supports his thesis.
5. What makes the essay interesting? (List 3 or 4 specific items.)

HOW TO FIND TIME
by Dale Turner

1.   A commercial flashing on our TV screens shows men and women trying to buy a bit of time. It catches the plight of most of us in our hurry-scurry world. "I don't want a 4O-hour week," says Nicholas Murray Butler, former president of Columbia University. "I want a 40-hour day."

2.   I never cease to marvel at how some people, working with the same number of hours we have, seem to get so much more done. How do they do it?

3.   For one thing, they don't squander the bits and pieces of time that punctuate our days. Rather than wasting energy getting irritated waiting for a phone call or a repair person, they capture those moments creatively. They keep tools handy--a pen, a book, a pair of scissors, a needle, whatever.

4.   Clement C. Moore was a teacher of classical languages. In the course of his career, he published a Hebrew dictionary and was a major benefactor of the General Theological Seminary in New York City.

5.   But it is not for the seminary or his dictionary that he is remembered. It is for a set of verses dashed off in 1822 in an hour of yuletide inspiration--verses that he stuffed away as if of no importance.

6.   The magic lines begin: "'Twas the night before Christmas, and all through the house

..." They never brought Moore a penny, but they did bring him immortality.

7.   Such constructive use of time is available to us all. A Seattle businessman carries a briefcase in which he has paper and envelopes for penning letters. In odd moments he keeps countless friendships alive.

8.   A woman I know memorized the Sermon on the Mount while commuting. A bedspread in our home was quilted by my mother-in-law who, though extremely busy, found minutes to prepare a beautiful gift full of memories for her family.

9.   Remember, most time is wasted in minutes, not hours. The average person diddles away enough minutes in ten years to have earned a college degree.

10.   Thinking of this reminds me of a verse from my childhood by Julia Fletcher Carney:

Little drops of water,
Little grains of sand,
Make the mighty ocean
And the pleasant land.

Do you recall the next four lines?

So the little minutes,
Humble though they be,
Make the mighty ages
Of eternity.

Used by permission

WRITING THE ESSAY, STEP BY STEP

THE DESCRIPTIVE ESSAY

A well-written essay is not a goal that can be achieved in one sitting, like completing a math lesson or history assignment. When you start on such a project, you should expect it to stretch over three to five days. Some of the assignments later in this book will take longer. This allows time for your thoughts to shake out and settle in a way that makes sense, both to you and to your reader.

In my writing classes I use an acronym called TOWER. It looks like this:

T hink

O rganize

W rite

E valuate

R ewrite

Organizing and expressing thoughts is a process of moving forward, adding ideas, backing up, and starting over--it's more like a shopping expedition at the Mall than a journey from A to B. So it's wise to start a writing assignment with the *expectation* that you're going to wander, explore, and backtrack. I will break the process into steps to make it easier to handle. Read all five steps on the next four pages and schedule your first essay assignment. The entire project should take no more than a week.

> ASSIGNMENT. Write a descriptive essay (one to two pages long) of a person, place or object of special significance to you. Your goal will be to communicate *why* the subject of your essay is special. Allow one day for each step.

STEP ONE -THINK

This assignment comes with a ready-made topic: the person, place or object you choose to describe. Since the topic is defined, you can skip the clustering step.

The thesis statement will be a declaration of why that person, place, or object is special to you. It must be as specific as possible (have you heard this before?). Each of the sentences below is too general to make an engaging thesis statement, and here's why:

1. Palisades Park is my favorite summertime hangout.
   (This will probably lead to a list of items in the park that the writer likes--with the result that it quickly begins to sound like every other park!)

2. Aunt Sophie is my favorite relative.
   (Same problem: a picture of a nice lady who could be anybody.)

3. This glove and I have been through a lot together.

   ("Being through a lot together" could include just about anything, from the time the dog buried it in the yard to the time you used it as an egg basket.)

4. My brother is fun to be around.

   (Does this include the time he told that cute tennis instructor you had Tourette's syndrome?)

5. I like my room.

   (As in the first example, this could lead to another list of items; you may as well be writing a furniture catalogue.)

All of these sentences can be improved by making them more specific. How do we accomplish this? Observe:

1. Palisades Park is the place where I learned to love swimming.
2. The softness of Aunt Sophie's touch and warmth of her hands have comforted me many times in my life.
3. This trusty baseball glove has scored more than one tie-breaking catch.
4. Everyone perks up when they hear my brother's laugh, because he's always the life of the party.
5. My bedroom is the one place where I can relax and just be me.

Notice that each of these sentences isolates *one* quality that makes the subject special to the writer. This will automatically tighten up the essay, for everything in it must, in some way, support the thesis statement. Notice also that each sentence manages to communicate that quality without saying, "This person [or place or object] is special to me because . . ." Being specific is not the same as being obvious.

Think carefully about the object of your description. Then write a thesis statement that *a)* specifies one quality or characteristic, and *b)* communicates the special quality of your subject in an indirect way.

STEP TWO: ORGANIZE

This is the step most often neglected by young writers who just want to get the assignment over with. But a short investment of time at this stage can save an hour or more of staring at a blank piece of paper. Reserve a page in your notebook for organizing, a process we will divide into two stages.

1. Expand on the ideas expressed in your thesis statement. Rewrite the sentence in different words. Do you discover any further shades of meaning? Make a short list of incidents or examples that illustrate your thesis statement. Think of sensory details that can bring the object of your description into sharp focus. What sounds, colors, or textures are associated with this person or place? Does a certain smell or a special song bring it to mind? Make a list of sensory impressions associated with your subject--you may wish to

set up five columns headed by the five senses, and write at least one detail for each.

2. During the first stage of organizing, you were writing down memories and impressions as quickly as they came to you. Now give your scribbled thoughts a second look. First of all, consider your thesis statement. Perhaps the ideas you wrote down have led you in a different direction and the sentence no longer expresses the main idea of your essay. If so, rewrite it. Then review all your supporting ideas and sensory details. You should have more than you need, so cross out any details you don't like or any thoughts that don't fit.

All this thinking should have given you an idea of how to arrange your material. Rather than simply piling on details, choose a pattern of organization, such as side to side or general to specific (see p. 34). After you've decided on a logical sequence for your essay, number your ideas in the order that you plan to use them.

Here's an example of an organizing page for a descriptive essay. Notice how some of the details are crossed out because they don't add anything to the thesis.

```
Thesis Statement: Palisades Park is where I learned to love
    swimming.
Rewritten: The smell of chlorine will always remind me of summer.
Sense details:                    Locality: general to specific,
chlorine smell                    getting near the pool
bright aqua color                 Incident, actions:
icy water                         1. approach to the park
blare of radios                      getting a snack
kids shouting                     3. bouncing on the low dive
tingling skin                     4. getting into the water
biting taste of Pepsi             1. sounds, smells of pool.
bare feet on the sidewalk
```

STEP THREE -WRITE

With a clear thesis statement and plenty of details to work with, you should have no problem getting started. You may type your first draft or write in longhand, but whether typed or written, remember to double-space. That is, skip every other line. If using a word processing program, set the paragraphing format for double-space. This is important to remember: ALL college papers and submitted manuscripts are to be double-spaced, so that corrections and changes can be easily added between the lines. Make it a habit!

When writing your first draft, follow these guidelines:

1. Include your thesis statement, word for word. It may occur anywhere in the description: beginning, middle, or end.
2. Every sentence should in some way support the thesis statement (expand on it, build up to it, or explain it).
3. Include *lots* of specific detail to make the object of your essay come alive for the reader.

Now write your description in a logical order, using the supporting ideas and details. If any brilliant thoughts occur to you while you're writing, feel free to include them! When you think you're finished, put the essay aside and don't look at it for at least 24 hours.

ABOUT COMPUTERS: Contrary to popular belief, a word processing program will not necessarily help you write better. The same steps and the same brain work apply, whether you tackle the assignment with a pencil or on a keyboard. That said, however, a computer does eliminate much of the tedious work of revising and rewriting (steps four and five). I write almost all my first drafts in longhand (double-spaced), than make revisions and type it on a word-processing program for further revision. If you have a computer, I suggest you learn to type (assuming you haven't already) and make use of it for something besides fun and games.

STEP FOUR: EVALUATE

Now you get to polish your rough-cut diamond. **Revision** is the process of looking over your work to decide where improvements can be made--anything from changing a single word to rearranging or deleting whole sentences. In revision, it's helpful to "step back" from your work as far as possible; that's why you waited at least 24 hours before going back to it. Don't wait more than two or three days, however, or you may never go back!

The first question to ask yourself is this: does the description succeed in its goal (to make the reader understand precisely *why* this person, place or object is so important to me)? You may decide, after rereading, that some element is missing. The picture isn't as complete as you thought, or the sentences don't hang together as well as they should. Ask yourself the following questions to help identify the problem:

CONTENT QUESTIONS:
1. Did you follow your organizational plan (or did you even *use* an organizational plan)?
2. Are any of the sentences confusing? Too long? Awkwardly put together? (If so, rewrite them.)
3. Does every sentence relate in some way to the thesis statement? (Cross out the ones that don't, or change them so that they do.)
4. Are there enough sensory details to help the reader "see" the person, place or object being described? (If not, add more--sensory details are crucial to descriptive writing.)

The next set of questions will help you address matters of style.

STYLE QUESTIONS
1. Do too many of your sentences sound alike? Too many begin with "he," "she," or "it"? Can you rearrange the monotonous sentences, or combine the short ones?
2. Can you replace any bland or linking verbs with strong action verbs? Can any nouns be more specific?

3. Can any sentences be rewritten for emphasis, either by word order, repetition or parallel structure? (Pay special attention to the last sentence.)
4. Can you cross out any unnecessary words--meaningless phrases, repetitions or clichés?
5. Do you hear any "echoes"--repeated words or phrases?

Once you've corrected all the style and content errors, check for mechanical errors such as spelling, punctuation and grammar.

Below is a revision of our sample essay. If you study it carefully you should get a feel for some of the changes that might be necessary in your own revision.

Just a short walk from my house is
Palisades Park, ~~is just a short walk from my house.~~ On hot | Rearrange first sentence for emphasis

summer days I spend almost every afternoon there, and most

of them in the water. The pool is where I learned to love
tingling
swimming. The ᵥchlorine smell reaches me even before I cross | Add descriptive details
blaring
the street to get to the park. Shouting children and ᵥradios
indicate
~~are the next indication~~ that I'm getting nearer. My skin | Replace linking verb with action verb

tingles in anticipation of the cold, clear water as I slip

off my sandals and T-shirt and make a beeline for the low
The *go-splat! splat!*
dive. ~~I hear the~~ bare feet of kids on the wet concrete as | Let the reader "hear"!

they try to hurry without running ₍and attracting the | Omit--slows down the action

attention of the lifeguard₎ Usually there's not a ⟨long⟩ line | Omit one "long"
in a short time
at the low dive, and ~~I don't have to wait long before~~ I'm
of the board
balancing lightly on the edge. My arms go up, my body | Add phrase for clarity

curves and with a little spring I arch from the board and
slice *plunge*
~~enter~~ the water. I break the surface again and ~~throw my~~ | Use a strong verb here

body forward in a strong freestyle. No matter how many

times I go to the pool, that first dive is always a thrill.

Next year I'll probably have a job and won't be able to come
pool
to the ~~Park~~ as often, but the smell of chlorine will always
remind me
~~be a reminder~~ of summer, *and Palisades Park.* | Replace the noun with a verb

STEP FIVE -REWRITE

This step will be the easiest of all, especially if you typed your first draft in a word-processing program. If you didn't, you face a tedious job, but not a difficult one. The reason for the rewrite, of course, is to put your writing in a form that someone besides you can read. Communication with others is the whole point. Type or print out the essay and be sure to let your teacher (and one other person) read it.

THE NARRATIVE ESSAY

The next assignment will require the same steps, but we'll be using them to write a different type of essay. Again, allow no more than a week for all five steps.

> ASSIGNMENT. Write a narrative essay, three or four paragraphs long, about an experience that taught you a lesson.

The centerpiece of a narrative essay is a story--often a story from the writer's personal experience. Not all narrative essays are about the lessons of life--some are designed to illustrate a point the author wants to make; others attempt to: arouse a strong emotional response; still others are written mostly for laughs. But almost all of them have a purpose beyond merely sharing the writer's experience. Your purpose should be clear from the assignment: you are to write about an experience that made you a wiser, kinder, or otherwise better person.

STEP ONE -THINK

Here again, your topic is defined and there's no need to go clustering for it. The first task goes on inside your head---to sort through the huge amount of experiences you have had and select one that taught you something. This "something" needn't be profound. Perhaps you merely learned not to provoke a kid who outweighs you by fifty pounds or not to eat Cracker Jacks underwater. But the lesson should involve a larger principle that any reader would understand, such as a healthy respect for muscle power or the value of common sense.

On a clean page in your notebook, summarize the experience in a short paragraph. Then write a general thesis, stating the universal lesson you learned, followed by your thesis sentence making it plain how the lesson applied in your personal experience. For example, suppose you decided to write about a frightening experience with the family mini-van . . .

```
Summary:  When my little sister needed a ride home from
choir practice I volunteered to pick her up, even though
Mom was worried about the snow that was beginning to fall.
I picked up Christy without mishap but right away she
```

started pushing me to drive faster. Wanting to show off,
I decided on a daredevil plunge down "Suicide Hill" and
ended up sliding the mini-van into a ditch.
General Thesis: Teenagers can be pretty cocky about their
new independence until reality takes them down a peg.
Thesis Sentence: A beginning driver has to learn respect
for nature--too bad he usually learns from experience.

Your own thesis sentence might read something like this:

1. Apologizing to my brother was one of the hardest things I ever
   did, but it cleared the bad feelings between us like magic.
2. Most of all, I learned never to sneak up on my dad while he's
   hanging a light fixture.
3. I decided that the look on Mandie's face when I gave her my
   ticket was almost as much fun as going to Disneyland myself.

STEP TWO -ORGANIZE

On the same sheet of paper, list some of the sensory details of this experience: what
you saw, heard, touched, smelled, etc. These details won't be as important as they were in
the descriptive essay, but selective use of them will make your narrative more interesting
to the reader.

After listing your sensory impressions, write the events of the experience in the
order that they happened. This will accomplish two purposes. First, it will help you keep
your narrative understandable; second, it will help you focus on the crucial moment, or
climax of your story. The "events" list for my mini-van adventure might look like this:

first snow of the season   approach to Suicide Hill
Christy needs a ride   I decide to speed up--disaster!
I volunteer; Mom's warning   sickening feeling as car goes
easy drive to school   out of control
Christy's dare   the result: bent axle, bent
skid on corner: warning   pride, bent bank account

Almost half of the events are about the approach and descent down Suicide Hill.
That is the crucial moment, and at least half the essay should focus on it. Many of the
other items are necessary for setting the scene, but will not have so important a place in the
narrative. Some may not even be worth mentioning at all.

STEP THREE -WRITE

Your draft should tell the story with enough detail to make it interesting, but not so
much that the all-important focus is lost. Double-space, and follow these guidelines:

1. Write a paragraph that explains, in general terms, the "universal lesson" you learned. You will not necessarily use this paragraph as first written; you may decide to break it up and scatter key sentences throughout the essay, or use it as part of your introduction, or save it for the conclusion.
2. Include enough background material to help the reader understand the setting.
3. Use strong verbs whenever possible.
4. Work in those sensory details.
5. Use at least one direct quote, or brief dialogue.
6. Include your thesis statement, in its original or a slightly altered form.
7. Break your narrative into paragraphs. Short paragraphs should come at the climax of the narrative and/or at the conclusion.

STEP THREE-AND-A-HALF - THE INTRODUCTORY PARAGRAPH

If you were asked to introduce a speaker at a meeting, you would try to learn something about the speaker first. Why? Because you want to create audience interest in the speaker. Because you want to let the audience know what to expect. And because you want to avoid looking like an idiot. For the same reasons (except the last), it's a good idea to wait until the body of the draft is finished *before* writing the introductory paragraph. You will know exactly what's coming so you'll know how to create interest and inform the reader without giving too much away. Though it may seem backward to write the first paragraph last, the idea should make sense to you once you've practiced it.

Writers know several techniques for creating interest. Here are three that are especially adaptable to narrative essays:

* Begin with a quote.

> "Great!" Mom exclaimed, as she set down the phone receiver with floury hands. "Your sister's choir rehearsal broke up early, and I'm in the middle of a huge baking project."

* Begin in the middle of the action.

> One of the scariest sensations a driver can have is feeling 2000 pounds of sheet metal and rubber slide out of control on an icy hill.

* Begin with a foreshadowing statement.

> I had only had my driver's license for five months, but my record was spotless. What's a little snow to a perfect driver?

Choose an approach that works for your narrative, then write an introductory paragraph. Put the essay aside for at least twenty-four hours.

STEP FOUR - EVALUATE

When you come back to the essay after a day or two, read it with a fresh mind. Since this is a different type of essay from descriptive, we will add one more content question: Is the narrative interesting, clear, and understandable?

If you sense any confusion, do some troubleshooting in these areas:

a. Check the sequence to make sure you told everything in order .
b. Add any time or space transitions that might help explain the action, such as *after they left, over by the Coke machine, when she said that,* etc.
c. Add any details or linking sentences that would fill the gaps in understanding.
d. Make sure you kept the focus and left out all details and actions that were not relevant to the main event.
e. Make sure that the broader application (or "universal lesson") is clear.

Once you're confident that *anyone* could understand your narrative, continue with the style questions on pages 60-61.

STEP FIVE -REWRITE

Now put it together with the introductory paragraph. Type or print your narrative with all corrections and additions, then let your teacher read it. If you've followed the procedure carefully, he or she should be impressed. Here's an example of a revised narrative essay, with the introduction added:

> One of the scariest sensations a driver can ever have is feeling 2000 pounds of sheet metal and rubber slide out of control on an icy hill. If the driver is only sixteen, it's a humbling experience as well.
> How do I know that? Let's just say it wasn't so long ago that I was sixteen and possessed a perfect driving record. True, I hadn't had my license for very long, but as soon as a teenager makes one of those giant steps toward independence, he's inclined to get a little over-confident. One cold night in December, my mom received a telephone call from my sister Christy, who needed a ride home from choir practice. Since my dad was out of town on a business trip and Mom was in the middle of a marathon Christmas-cookie-baking project, I volunteered to pick her up.
> "Well . . ." Mom glanced out the window. "I don't know, Sam. It looks like that snow we were expecting has already started. You've never driven in snow before."
> I managed to convince her that I would never get experience driving in snow without driving in snow, and soon after was backing the mini-van out of the garage. Like a

good Drivers' Ed. student, I drove <u>slowly</u> all the two miles
to school. This isn't so bad, I thought as I pulled into the
parking lot.

When she flopped into the front seat, Christy said,
"What took you so long?"

"It's snowing--duh!"

"So what? Are you scared?"

As sisters go, Christy can be fun, but she doesn't
always think things through. To be honest, maybe I wasn't
thinking too clearly either, because once on the road again I
bumped up my speed just a little. The snow was diving at the
windshield like tiny parachutes. But it was dry and fluffy,
and the tires seemed to plow right though it. Rounding the
corner from Sparks Boulevard onto Lambert Street, I felt the
rear wheels skid slightly, but they soon straightened out. I
was beginning to wonder what all the fuss was about.

"Hey, look!" Christy exclaimed. "Suicide Hill coming
up. Let's pretend we're sledding."

"Suicide Hill," about half a mile from our house,
wasn't very long, but it was pretty steep. I made a careful
considered judgment--yes, the road was getting slicker, but
so what if we skidded a little as long as the van went
straight? I pushed the accelerator a fraction as the
headlights swung down to point at the slope.

I felt the surge in speed immediately. "Cool!" Christy
yelled, but I was already pushing down on the brake pedal.
Then I realized the wheels weren't rolling--they were
sliding. Uh-oh, I thought.

The mini-van aimed for the ditch at the bottom of the
hill, and I couldn't do anything about it. My efforts to
steer away from certain doom only swiveled the car sideways,
like a smart-alecky kid who turns his back and refuses to do
what you say. "Look out!" Christy screamed, as the back
wheels came to rest over the edge of the culvert.

I was furious: "Look what you made me do!"

Of course, the person I was really mad at was me. By
the time we got through yelling at each other, and a passing
motorist gave us a lift home and Mom called the tow truck,
and we discovered that the rear axle was bent, I understood
where all the blame belonged. Every beginning driver learns
to have respect for nature. It's too bad he has to learn
from experience.

EXPOSITORY ESSAYS

The Latin word *exponere,* from which we get "expository," means "to set forth." The goal of expository writing is to set forth information for a reader, in newspaper and magazine articles, textbooks, travelogues, biographies, owner's manuals, and expository essays.

An expository essay is often more personal in tone than a magazine or newspaper article, but still the facts take center stage. The impressions, feelings, and opinions of the writer may pop up here and there, but the main purpose of exposition is to inform the reader on a given topic.

Most students have done at least some expository writing by the time they get to high school. Every "report" you were assigned, from a biographical sketch of Thomas Jefferson to a paper on the food pyramid, required you to seek out facts on the subject and organize them into a short, readable format.

JUST THE FACTS

When you are asked to write about something you already know (such as "How to Deliver the Perfect Tennis Serve," or "Antique Snuffbox Collecting for Fun and Profit"), the facts are already in your head although you may wish to look up a few technical terms or statistics. But for most expository writing assignments, in school and out, you will have to do some research in order to get the facts.

You are probably familiar with the sources known to every grade schooler: encyclopedias and library books. As you grow older, however, teachers and parents seem to expect more of you (you've probably noticed this already). They used to be satisfied if you read two encyclopedia articles on the battle of Gettysburg and wrote a two-page report, but when you reach high school and college they want more sources, and different types of sources, and sources that can't be taken out of the library (which means you have to sit there for *hours* taking notes). At some stage in your academic career a 20-page term paper is lurking. The whole point of such papers is to teach you to find and organize facts.

The feasibility studies in Part One gave you some experience with practical research, in which the goal was to gather information for decision-making. Now we will be exploring other areas of research. The goal is to find information in order to communicate it to others.

GETTING AT THE TRUTH

Shakespeare wrote a number of historical plays in which the historical facts were somewhat skewed. While it may be debatable whether this was justified, his main purpose was not to teach a history lesson but to create compelling drama. As long as the audience understands this, Shakespeare may be excused for occasionally manipulating history.

But in expository essays, the information *itself* is the most important element. That's why it's vital to get the facts straight. Remember this rhyme:

When in doubt,
Check it out
Or do without.

Now let's look at some of the places where facts can be found.

INFORMATION SOURCES

The Internet. Since the mid-1990s, the Internet has become the first stop for student researchers, but it's not always the best. Information on the Information Superhighway may be sketchy, incomplete, biased or even made up--after all, anyone can get a website and proclaim himself an expert. For historical and literary topics, the Internet is a poor resource. For current events and science topics it's much better, as long as the source is reliable. In general, it's best not to trust an individual's credentials unless there is some way to verify them. Material gained from the websites of institutions, newspapers or magazines are usually more reliable, as long as you take into consideration the particular "slant" that the organization may have.

Print. Print sources are by far the most varied and numerous. Whether on a computer screen or hard copy, you can find anything in print if you know where to look. In most cases, the first step is your local library. Larger libraries naturally contain more information, but even small libraries have their sources. The best way to find out what they are is to *ask*. This book can't tell you the research capacity of the library nearest you; it's your job to find out.

Your next assignment (see below) is to check out the reference section of the nearest library. Most have books of government-related information, such as state and federal offices, population and financial statistics, and legislative records. You may also find historic documents, atlases, local history records, yearbooks, indexes, bibliographies, even telephone directories.

> ASSIGNMENT. In the back of your notebook, make a list of reference works available in your local library. If the library is a large one, you will not want to list all the titles; instead, note the various *types* of references, plus titles of specific databases that are available to you. Talk to the librarian first. Since you never know what you may need, be sure you list references in all areas. After talking to the librarian, browse among the reference section and list titles that may be of specific interest to you. More than likely, you'll notice that reference books are arranged according to the Dewey decimal classification system, the same as the rest of the library's collection.

The Dewey Decimal System is the organizing scheme for the vast majority of public libraries. If you don't know a specific title for a subject that you're researching, it's often worthwhile to browse among the stacks in the area where that subject might be found. Not only does this limit your search to those books that are immediately available to you, but you'll be able to compare volumes and choose the ones which seem most helpful. This "grazing" can also help you focus your topic or lead you in an interesting direction you didn't foresee. On page 103 you'll find a detailed breakdown of the classifications in the Dewey system. If you know the classification number of the subject you're looking for, you can go directly to the stacks without taking time to look up the subject in the library's catalogue.

Periodicals. Periodicals are newspapers, newsletters and magazines--usually the best source when writing about science or current events topics. Here, unfortunately, most small-town libraries are not much help. But the larger libraries usually have a periodicals index, either in book form or on computer. Some even offer separate indexes for broad subjects such as medicine and health, business, or local history. As you probably know, many periodicals post current articles on their Internet websites, though you may have to pay for articles drawn from their archives.

The periodicals themselves may be in their original form, or bound between hard covers, or compressed on microfilm or microfiche (which has to be read on a special machine). Usually these items can't be checked out, but most libraries have photocopiers, which will allow you to copy the pages you need. If you're wondering about copyright laws, the "fair use" guidelines allow you to copy one entire article up to 2500 words, or a 1000-word excerpt of a longer article or book. The information is for your use only; you can't make copies and sell them!

Oral Resources. You may have read newspaper or magazine articles which introduced new facts with the words "authorities say" or "according to the experts . . ." This usually means that the writer has tracked and cornered such a person and asked him or her to give an opinion. An "authority" is one who holds a certain position and can be expected to know something about the field in which he or she works. In the media, an "expert" is usually a person with at least one PhD degree--who may or may not have much practical knowledge. In everyday terms, we understand that an expert is someone with particular knowledge and/or experience in a given field.

If you think about it, you'll discover all kinds of experts, even in your own home. You yourself are probably an expert on something, whether bicycle repair or cross stitch or bowling. Such a person is an excellent resource, as long as he or she truly understands the subject. If you've ever asked your mother about baby care or questioned a sporting goods clerk about the best brand of in-line skates, you're familiar with this type of research. We call it "oral" research because it usually consists of asking questions of the source and writing down the spoken answers. It's a valid form of gathering facts for expository research as long as these guidelines are followed:

1. The source should be identified, along with his or her credentials (i.e., why this person may be considered an expert).
2. Any opinions expressed by the source should be identified as opinions.
3. All direct statements should be quoted word-for-word and placed in quotation marks.

If summarizing a statement by the source, quotation marks are not necessary. For example:

a. "That was the first time I met President Truman," Mr. Foulkes said.
b. Mr. Foulkes indicated that this incident was the first time he met President Truman.

ASSIGNMENT. Choose one of the following options, then write a short expository piece (3-6 paragraphs) about the topic.
1. Ask your father or another trusted adult to explain one of the toughest challenges he faces with his job.
2. Ask an athletic friend for his or her favorite fitness tips.
3. Ask an older friend with an interesting hobby about how to get started in that hobby.
4. Ask a traveling friend about the highlight of his or her latest trip.
5. Ask your local librarian how books are chosen for purchase.

Personal Experience/Observation. Investigative reporters often get personally involved in their research. They may make purchases in a store rumored to overcharge customers, or pose as a patient in a veterans' hospital in order to get the "scoop" first-hand. Travel writers go to faraway places and report on what they see and do. Sports writers attend games, and drama critics go to the theater. All these writers use their own observations as the foundation of their reports.

Now that we've taken a helpful side trip into available sources for research, it's time to get to work.

WRITING THE EXPOSITORY ESSAY

ASSIGNMENT. Write an expository essay of 3-5 double-spaced pages on any topic of interest to you. Use two or three print sources, (or two print and one oral source), research the topic and narrow the focus to a specific area before you start writing. Allow no more than two weeks for the entire assignment.

STEP ONE - GATHER INFORMATION

Since you will rely on sources other than yourself for this assignment, this step involves as much researching as thinking. As usual, I'll break the process into steps.

1. To get an overall view of the subject, read a general article on it, such as you would find in an encyclopedia or magazine. Draw a cluster diagram showing various aspects of the subject, then choose *one* to write about. For example, if you're interested in trout fishing you might browse through an angler's guide, cluster possible topics, and decide on "How to find the best fishing locations."

2. Write a tentative thesis statement. "Tentative" means you'll probably change it when you have more information, but even at this stage, try to make it as specific as possible. A thesis statement for the trout fishing essay might be, "At least half the sport of trout fishing lies in locating the perfect spot."

3. Now it's time to gather your sources. Since you've narrowed the topic, you can target your research to that specific area. For this assignment, you should locate two or three sources, and at least two of them should be print sources (such as an article in *Field and Stream*). If you know someone who is knowledgeable in this area, like a game warden or conservation agent, you may use him or her as an oral source. It's even permissible to use your own experience as a "source," *if* that experience can shed some real light on the topic. (If you've only spent an afternoon puttering around the creek with no new insights--or trout--to show for it, you would not make a good source!) Once you have your material, it's finally time for Step Two.

STEP TWO - ORGANIZE

1. Use your sources to get the information you need, practicing the note-taking techniques you learned in Part One of this book. Since this will be a relatively short essay, it won't be necessary to use note cards; a sheet of loose-leaf paper or a notepad will do.

2. In the light of all your new information; you may have to revise your thesis statement. To go back to our trout fishing example, it now seems that locating the ideal spot is even harder than we thought. We won't change much--just a few words to make the sentence more specific: "At least half the challenge of trout fishing lies in locating the ideal spot."

3. Make a formal outline. You have gathered information from two or three sources; now you must recombine these pieces of information into a unified whole. It's like shuffling a deck of cards after a solitaire game, when you pick up your suits and re-combine them. In the same way, you will "shuffle" bits of information from different sources into a new combination. Your outline will be a chart of this new combination, which will point you in the right direction when you begin writing. The outline need not be detailed. Something like the following would be adequate:

```
      I. Introduction: the difficulty
     II. Body
         A. "Think like a fish"
            1. food
            2. shelter
         B. Handling the currents
         C. Finding habitats
            1. trout habits
            2. recognizing the signs
    III. Conclusion: worth the trouble
         Silver Creek story
```

STEP THREE- WRITE

Now that you have your outline, this essay should write itself! Start directly on the "body" section, saving the introduction for last. A good rule of thumb would be to devote one paragraph to each upper-case letter in the body section of your outline--but be sure to break up paragraphs that involve a lot of detail. As you write, try to imagine a reader who is very interested in this topic (you can be sure there are some) and anticipate any questions he or she might have. As a matter of fact, *you* are presumably interested in this topic--what questions did *you* have? Observe these guidelines:

1. Follow your outline.

2. Use at least one direct quotation from one of your sources.

3. Avoid general statements in the body of the essay, such as, "Trout fishing is fun." If you are specific and interesting, the essay itself should get that point across. The only place for a general statement is in the conclusion.

4. Use the final paragraph to summarize the main point and state your personal feelings, if any.

When the body of the essay is completed, write the introductory paragraph. Some of the ideas for introducing a narrative essay may not be appropriate here. Consider these instead:

   a. Relate a personal experience relevant to this topic.
   b. Relate an experience from one of your sources.
   c. Quote a provocative comment you gathered from your research or your oral source.
   d. Comment from an unusual point of view (for example, a trout considering his priorities).

STEP FOUR - EVALUATE

Read over your essay for content. If the body of the essay makes sense and flows logically, continue with these corrections:

1. Insert references to show the origin of your sources. For example: "Dan Ewing ("Tracking the Slippery Silverback," Field and Stream, April 1998) claims that very few novices take this subject seriously."
2. Make sure all facts (names, dates, sequences, etc.) are correct.
3. Check your introduction: is it specific enough to create interest in the topic? Ask yourself if you would want to finish the essay, after reading only the introduction.

Now turn to page 60 and continue with style corrections.

STEP FIVE - REWRITE

Type or print your final draft, and let at least three people read it.

We're not through with expository essays yet!

> ASSIGNMENT. Choose a topic which will require an oral interview as your primary source, and write an expository essay 8-12 paragraphs long. Allow two weeks for this assignment.

STEP ONE - GATHER INFORMATION

The requirement that your *primary* source must be oral will limit you to people with whom you can meet personally. This assignment could stretch your circle of acquaintances! Once again, the research stage will be rather involved.

1. Unless you already have a topic and a resource person in mind, you will start with some brainstorming. Write down ideas as they come to you. To get the creative juices flowing, jot down answers for some of these categories:

Professions that interest me
Sports and recreations I'd like to try
Buildings in town that I like
Everything I know about local history
Everything I know about local politics
Local festivals and celebrations

New businesses
Items of interest in the neighborhood
    newspaper
Local notables (people who have done
    interesting things: authors, travelers, artists,
    collectors, etc.)

Once you have some names and topics on paper, do any of them look interesting to you? If so, mark two. If not, mark the two that seem least boring to you, or make up your own. For these two topics, make a "feasibility" plan answering these questions:

Whom should I talk to? (More than one person?)
How can I reach him or her?

2. As soon as possible, call this person to set up an interview. If it's someone you already know, this will be simple. If not, act professional. Introduce yourself and explain that you need information for a school assignment, that you are interested in what they know, and that you would appreciate half an hour of their time. Most experts love to talk about their field and will be glad to accommodate you, if possible. If it's not possible for them to meet you, go to the next topic on your list and call that contact person.

3. Even before the interview, you should know enough about the topic to a) ask intelligent, specific questions, and b) have a focus. Visit your local library for background information if necessary--check newspapers, magazines and encyclopedias.

4. Write a list of five to eight specific questions for your interview subject. Avoid open-ended questions, such as, "What can you tell me about [the topic]?" Your last question should be, "Can you recommend any books or articles I should read to learn more?"

5. With your list of questions, a pencil, and a notebook firmly in hand, arrive promptly for your appointment. Plan to take no more than a half-hour of your subject's time. Be friendly but respectful and get right to the point. If you bring a tape recorder to the interview, be sure to ask permission to use it (some people aren't comfortable being recorded, and besides, secret taping is illegal). Even if you use a recorder, be sure to take written notes in case of a malfunction. (My motto is, never trust a machine!) One more point: wandering off into discussion with your subject can be fascinating as well as informative, but be sure you get your questions answered in the given amount of time.

6. The interview should have clarified the direction of your essay. Write a focused and specific thesis statement.

7. Use one print source to provide information not covered in the interview. If your subject could recommend one, check into it. If not, use what you turned up at the library. A whole book is too much. A chapter or magazine article is more like it--even an encyclopedia article can provide valuable information for certain subjects.

STEP TWO - ORGANIZE

All that work, and we're only on step two! But the other steps are familiar territory by now. Combine the information from your print source with what you learned at the interview, then organize the material in an outline.

STEP THREE -WRITE

Once again, you will start directly on the body of the essay, leaving the introduction for later. Check the guidelines on pages 72, and follow your outline.

For an introduction, consider writing a short description of the person you interviewed. Include any details of the surroundings that relate to your essay topic. Another option is to begin with an interesting quote from your subject, followed by a transitional sentence to link it to the body of the essay.

STEP FOUR - EVALUATE

Revise your essay using the content guidelines on page 72 and style questions on pages 60-61.

STEP FIVE -REWRITE

After rewriting your essay, be sure to send a copy to your interview subject. You might also consider sending a copy to the local newspaper--they might print it!

We'll write one more expository essay before leaving this section. This time the major resource person will be you!

> ASSIGNMENT. Write an expository essay based on a field trip, vacation, research project, special camp or some other unique experience.

You may wonder how this type of exposition is different from the narrative essay. The main difference is in the *purpose*. Your narrative was supposed to illustrate an event that changed you in some way. Of course that's not the purpose of all narrative essays, but still the focus is almost always personal. With exposition, the focus is impersonal. *You* are not as important in this assignment as the experience itself. Think of yourself as an investigative reporter or travel writer. Your personal reactions will add human interest to the essay, but your reader will be even more interested in what you discovered.

You should write about something that's rather out of the ordinary for you, although it doesn't have to be exotic. A basketball clinic, a ballet, even a grocery shopping expedition would qualify, if these are things you do not normally do. If such an occasion is coming up in the next two months, there's your essay topic. Schedule it now.

STEP ONE - GATHER INFORMATION

Take a notebook along on this excursion to jot down your impressions. Your essay should focus on only one part of the experience; presumably the part that made the greatest impression on you. Since you're not sure what that will be when you start, plan to take *plenty* of notes.

Be careful to write down any relevant facts that you hear or read; your purpose, remember, is to pass on information, not just give an account of your exciting day. Pick up any free brochures, leaflets, fact sheets, or other information that may be available. Ask questions, if there is anyone around to answer them.

STEP TWO - ORGANIZE

Back home, look over your notes, draw a cluster diagram if it helps, and determine what part of the experience will be the focus of your essay. Be sure you have enough facts (not just impressions) to inform your reader on this topic.

Write your thesis sentence and a rough outline.

STEP THREE - WRITE

Write the body and conclusion of the essay first, following guidelines on page 72.

Write two introductory paragraphs, using different approaches. An effective technique might be a "teaser" question, which you will answer in the body of the essay. For example:

```
    What has four hands, laughs like a tuba and wears a
hairnet?  I didn't know either until I visited DiMaggio's
bakery.

    "Wouldn't you like to see Swan Lake?" my mother asked
expectantly.  "You know, the ballet?"  I hesitate to put
my first reaction on paper.
```

STEP FOUR - EVALUATE

After a day or two, check your essay against the content guidelines for expository writing (page 72). Then revise according to the style questions on pages 60-61.

STEP FIVE - REWRITE

Copy or type your essay, and consider sending it to a local publication or school newsletter. Expository writing of this type is often quite popular--if you've done a good job, don't be afraid to share it!

A WORD ABOUT RESEARCH PAPERS

Research papers, or term papers, have been a part of college composition courses ever since Freshman Comp. classes were invented. In addition, many college-level courses other than English require some kind of research paper or project. For this reason, college-bound high school students should write at least one research paper before graduation.

These projects fall into two categories. The first is purely factual, intended to relay lots of information on a narrow topic. The second demands the writer not only to assemble and communicate this information, but also to form an opinion about it, and then support that opinion. For example, instead of a paper on "Napoleon's Waterloo Campaign," an advanced history student might choose to write about "Napoleon's Three Classic Mistakes During the Waterloo Campaign." Instead of "The History of *Huckleberry Finn*," a literature student might decide to prove that "*Huckleberry Finn* is Not a Racist Novel."

The second approach is called "defending a thesis." Graduate students working on a Master's or Doctor's Degree are required to do this, both orally and in writing. The facts are vital to making their case, but the students must also be able to use elements of judgment and persuasion (which you will learn about in the next two sections).

Here are some ideas for research paper topics. The topics in the first column are purely expository, while the second column is more opinion-based. Choosing a topic is *the most important step in writing a paper*--it should be interesting to you, with adequate resources available, and suitable for developing a specific thesis.

The development of nutritional soy products	The negative effects of nutritional soy for women
The painting technique of Vincent van Gogh	The effect of van Gogh's work on twentieth-century painting
The childhood of C. S. Lewis	How Lewis' early life influenced his Narnia books
Naval Intelligence in World War II	How Naval Intelligence helped win World War II
The Battle of Chancellorsville	Why the Battle of Chancelorsville was the real turning point of the Civil War

"Writing The Research Paper" is too broad a subject for this book, but I do recommend that college-bound students write at least two such papers during the last two years of high school. The first half of *Wordsmith Craftsman* will help you with writing style, the section on expository essays is all you need to know about defining a topic and gathering information, and the next two sections (critical and persuasive) will help you with defending your thesis. The rest is a matter of form: taking notes on note cards, writing footnotes or endnotes, and making a bibliography. Any college handbook can give you information about this.

THE CRITICAL ESSAY

You may have known people who are excessively negative and seem to find fault with everything and everybody. We often describe such people as "critical." But when talking about the arts, to "criticize" just means to evaluate according to a standard--to point out the good as well as the bad. Much of art and literature **criticism** is scholarly and deals with works that have been around for years or centuries; it's written by professors, enthusiastic amateurs or students producing term papers. But a professional **critic**--of books, music, art, theater, or movies--writes about recent productions, evaluating the overall worth. An essay written by a critic is called a **review**.

Critical judgment is a valuable skill to develop, especially in the world we live in. We're saturated with media; surrounded by music and books and movies offered for our amusement, our enlightenment and especially our dollars. Condemning what's bad in these products is as important as praising what's good, and will help you determine the best use of your time and money. Whether or not you realize it, you already hold certain standards in your mind for judging the quality of a novel, movie or play. Here are just a few:

Positive qualities
Admirable, likable, or "real" characters
Information conveyed in an interesting way
Insightful about life and human nature
Entertaining: funny, suspenseful, gripping
Beautiful or evocative in style
True to life (or reflects your worldview)

Negative qualities
Unsympathetic or unlikable characters
Trite and predictable; illogical
Preachy and condescending
Boring, confusing, overly violent or vulgar
Loaded with cliché; awkward and clumsy
Tries to make its case deceptively

Learning to write good criticism is a way to sharpen your perceptions of these criteria and develop sound judgment.

The review section of a newspaper or magazine is often the place I turn to first, because I'm interested how people think. I often find that the critic's opinion is very different from mine. This might be because he or she has seen something in the work that I missed, or else is evaluating from a different set of standards. But a well-written review always contains food for thought, even if I don't like the taste. The critic doesn't just write, "This is a great movie. Go see it." He or she will try to *prove* the point by appealing to certain standards and providing evidence why the work does or does not live up to them.

That's why writing a review may be more of a challenge than you think. It's not enough to "really love" a book or movie--you must understand *why* you love it (or hate it, if that's the case). Some pitfalls of critical writing for beginners are

* getting bogged down in retelling the story (a blow-by-blow account of the plot, rather than an evaluation of the whole work).

* trying to address too many issues (turning the review into a list of the critic's opinion on every aspect of the work--a quick trip to Monotony).

* being too vague or general--amounting to "This is a great book (movie, CD). You really ought to read (see, buy) it!"

Read and compare these two reviews:

Space Rebels is the stupidest science fiction movie I've ever seen. It takes place aboard a star-cruiser somewhere in "deep space." The crew is fed up with their sanctimonious captain and a couple of bad guys plan to revolt. They form an alliance with pirate mutants who promise to come to their aid when the time is right. Meanwhile, a space pod full of beautiful aliens is captured by the crew and kept in a holding cell where they transmit mysterious messages to officers aboard the cruiser. These officers try to investigate and are picked off one by one by the mutineers. As the body count grows, even the top-ranking officers get the idea that something is wrong, but it takes a hot-shot space pilot to figure out who the culprits are. The audience knows all along, of course.
　　The acting is lame, the special effects are cheesy, the dialogue is clunky and the plot makes no sense. Save your money.

Space Rebels demonstrates all the dangers of trying to make money by throwing together a low-budget knock-off of a popular genre. As the story opens, our heroes on a huge umpteenth-century star cruiser come under attack by enemy spacecraft (where have we seen that before?). The plot thickens--as thick as pea soup, in fact, as alien "goddesses," hostile pirates, a diabolical villain, and sadistic henchmen complicate matters. A hunky pilot and the captain's spunky daughter eventually save the day.
　　The special effects are anything but special, and the actors all seem to have been recruited from other occupations-- in fact, I'm sure the hero used to be a linebacker for some college bowl team. But the chief offense is careless construction. It's as if every space-movie cliché since Star Wars was thrown into a big pot and then served up half-cooked. Where are these enemy "pirates" we keep hearing about? They never appear. A communications officer is killed by the mutineers, yet shows up as an extra in the next scene. The aliens captured early in the film are supposed to have telekinetic powers but they seem to be there only to add mystical "depth." It all adds up to an insult to the movie-goer: how dumb do they think we are?

Notice how the writer of the first review fell into all three pitfalls: re-telling the plot, reducing the criticisms to a mere list, and not backing them up with evidence. The second review communicates enough of the plot to let the reader know what to expect, but focuses on one major complaint and supports it with three specific examples.

> ASSIGNMENT. Plan to see a movie or attend a play, and write a cinema or theater review, 1-2 double-spaced pages long. NOTE: Reviews are based on recent works, but plays are a special case. Live theater is so open to the director's interpretation that every time a play is produced it's considered a "new work"--even if Shakespeare wrote it 400 years ago!

STEP ONE - THINK

Keep a notebook handy while you watch, and jot down your reactions as they occur. Since the action won't stop for you, you have little time to sort out your responses. You'll probably write down impressions that you won't use, but try to keep the following questions in mind:

1. What's the main point (or is there one)?
2. How are lighting, music and cinematography (such as fast cuts, long-range shots, close-ups) used to create a mood or produce emotion?
3. Do you find yourself more interested in the characters or in the action?
4. How is humor used--to relieve tension, to provoke ridicule or to create sympathy for a character?
5. Can you use any part of this movie or play as a springboard to talk about religious or moral beliefs, or cultural values?

Just answering these questions should give you plenty of material!

STEP TWO - ORGANIZE

You should start organizing your impressions as soon as possible. First, determine whether your review will be positive or negative overall. This might not be as obvious as it seems. Rarely do I absolutely hate or absolutely love a movie--more often I find positive and negative elements and it may be hard to determine the balance. Once you've decided, list reasons for your overall judgment. Then determine the main reason for your opinion and list examples from the production that support it. An organizing page for the second review of *Space Rebels* might look like this:

```
Overall: BAD!
Reasons why: 1. Actors couldn't act
             2. Sloppy production
             3. You call those effects "special"?!
             4. Dialogue was corny
Evidence (for #2):
     Where were these "pirates"?
     What purpose did the alien mystics serve?
     That girl who was killed and showed up in the next
     scene!
```

STEP THREE - WRITE

In the first paragraph, explain briefly what the movie or play is about, without giving details of the plot. The first paragraph should also include some idea of whether your response was positive or negative.

For the next 1-3 paragraphs (depending on how long you wish to rant or rave), give specific reasons from the production itself why you came to the conclusions you did. Remember that word *specific*--a principle so important it's worth another example:

```
Too general:  The dialogue was stupid.
Much better:  The scriptwriter appeared to be drawing from
    a grab bag of "great movie lines."

Too general:  The action sequences were exciting.
Much better:  During the battle scene there was so much
    going on, I didn't know where to look.
```

The conclusion need be only 1-2 sentences, summing up your opinion. Unless the review takes a serious tone, you can end it with a catchy one-liner. For instance: "The only possible use I can see for this movie is as a non-addictive cure for insomnia."

STEP FOUR - EVALUATE

Reread your review after a day and ask yourself these questions:

1. Do I still agree with my own judgment, or would I change a few minor points?
2. Is there enough plot information to inform the reader what the movie/play is about?
3. Do I give away too much of the plot?
4. Do I maintain the focus on one (or at the most, two) major points, or does this review become a list?
5. Do I support my opinion with evidence from the production itself?

Continue your revision with style questions on pages 60-61.

STEP FIVE - REWRITE

Make your revisions and type or print a final copy. It would be interesting to compare your review with others that appear in the newspaper or on the Internet. You'll find there's a wide range of opinion! If you think you've done a good job, consider sending the review to your local newspaper or a teen website.

Now we'll turn from watching to reading.

> ASSIGNMENT. Write a critical essay (2-3 pp., double-spaced) of a novel you have read recently. It doesn't have to be a new book. In fact, it can be one you have read before, but you'll have to read it again for the essay.

Sometime in your school career, you probably had to write a book **report**. In writing a report, you don't necessarily have to express your opinion of the book--all you have to do is include enough information to prove you've read it. That usually means recounting the plot. A **critical essay**, as you should guess by now, delves below the surface of the plot in order to evaluate the overall quality of the book, or compare some aspect of it with other works.

So be prepared: you will not only have to read, you'll also have to think!

STEP ONE - THINK

Criticizing a book is easier in some ways than reviewing a movie or play because you have time to respond: to note your impressions of the language, flip back a few pages to make a comparison, or reread a confusing passage. But in another way it's more difficult because reading is a rational activity that takes place entirely inside your head. Dramas, especially movies, are more emotional. They go right for the senses--particularly visual and aural--and aim first at provoking an emotional response. A book doesn't give you those sensory clues; your imagination has to do all the work. While reading, ask yourself

1. What's the author's main point?
2. How does he or she get that point across (for example, by creating sympathy for or against certain characters)?
3. What's the mood of the book--serious, angry, light-hearted, ironic?
4. Does the author spend time developing characters (through flashbacks or other means), or is he or she more interested in moving the story along?
5. Do the characters seem like people you might actually meet? Do you find yourself still thinking about them after you've set the book aside for a while?
6. Do any elements of plot strike you as false--not true to life? For instance, do you sense the characters acting contrary to their personalities in order to produce a particular plot twist, or do the incidents of the story develop naturally from the personalities?
7. Do you gain any insights about life or human nature from this book?
8. Can you gain any insight into the author's philosophy or worldview?

STEP TWO - ORGANIZE

Critical essays often attempt to answer a particular question, such as, "How much do the witches influence the action in *Macbeth*?" For this assignment, the question you need to answer is, "Why do I like (or dislike) this book?" List specific positives and negatives, then determine whether your reaction is positive or negative overall. Decide on two main attributes to discuss in your review. They can be the things you liked most, the things you disliked most, or one of each. When you've decided on two points to address, list at least two examples from the book to support them.

STEP THREE - WRITE

Tell what the story is about in your first paragraph, again without simply summarizing the whole plot. You might also mention a few minor strengths or weaknesses of the novel before getting into your two main points.

For the next 4-6 paragraphs, focus on your primary likes and or dislikes. Remember to be specific (do I still have to say that?), as illustrated in these examples:

```
Too general:  I didn't like Callie at first, but ended up
    admiring her.
Much better:  Callie uses her father's death as an excuse
    for bad behavior, but at the end she's grown into a
    person capable to risking her life to save her sister.

Too general:  Mr. Pullman makes his case deceptively.
Much better:  Mr. Pullman "stacks the deck" by making all
    the church members evil, and all the rebels good.
```

Conclude with a strong statement of your overall judgment--again, more specific than "This is a great book!" Better to say, "This novel is a worthy addition to time travel literature," or "In spite of many imaginative passages and exciting scenes, I finished the trilogy with the sense that I had been through an attempted brainwashing."

STEP FOUR - EVALUATE

Give the essay a day to percolate, then read it with the content questions on page 81 in mind. Complete your revision with the style questions on pages 60-61.

STEP FIVE - REWRITE

The author of the book (if still living) might like to read your review, especially if it's positive. Look back at the "fan letter" section on page 14 for ideas on getting an address. You might also consider posting your review on Amazon.com or a book review website.

THE ART OF PERSUASION

Most of us hold convictions. That is, we're convinced that some things are true, and others are false. Below are several **assertions**, or statements of truth. With some you will agree, with others you won't, and for some you may have no opinion or can't judge without further information. Which is which?

1. Vinyl records deliver better sound quality than CD's.
2. Ronald Reagan was one of our greatest presidents.
3. Australia is the world's smallest continent.
4. International terrorism is currently the greatest threat to civilization.
5. Yeast dough needs a warm place in which to rise.
6. For traveling short distances, ten-speed bikes are best.
7. Married men live approximately twelve years longer, on average, than divorced men or bachelors.
8. Accessing the Internet is vital if you want to find out what's really going on in the world.
9. Individuals should be allowed to do whatever they want as long as no one else is hurt.
10. Electric heat is much more energy-efficient than natural gas.
11. Red-headed people usually have freckles.
12. Personal charity is not the job of the federal government.

You probably noticed that some of these assertions would be very easy to prove while others would be much harder. The reason is that even though all twelve statements make a point, they don't make the same *kind* of point. If we classified them according to type, they would fall into three categories:

a. **Empirical**. Empirical statements are based on evidence or observation. Statements 3, 5, 7, 10, and 11 fit this category, and are easy to prove as long as we have the facts.

b. **Pragmatic**. These are based on whatever seems to work best (statements 1, 6, and 8). Pragmatic assertions are harder to prove than empirical because we often have to rely on our own experience. Those who don't share our experience won't necessarily be impressed with our arguments. For example, if I love my 18-speed bike, your arguments for the 10-speed wouldn't go far with me. Likewise, well-educated and experienced people stand on both sides of the "how much should we rely on the Internet" question. A conclusion is usually based on individual preferences or needs.

c. **Moral/philosophical**. Morality concerns what is *right;* philosophy concerns what is *true*. They almost always go together because an individual's moral code is usually built upon what he or she believes to be true. If I believe that Reagan was a great President, it's because I share many of his philosophical beliefs about government and American values. Statements 2, 4, 9, and 12 are based on a philosophical foundation. These statements are the hardest to prove, because in order to convince someone who disagrees, you must bring him or her over to your basic worldview. Often, this is impossible.

EXERCISE. Write five statements that make an empirical point, five that make a pragmatic point, and five that make a philosophical point. Study the examples and definitions on the previous page before you start.

In a review or critical essay, the writer states an opinion. Persuasive essays are also statements of opinion, but more is at stake. The writer wants as many readers as possible to come to his or her point of view--or at least to think about it. If you go see that movie I recommended last week, I might be pleased, but I would be thrilled if you were persuaded by my arguments to vote for my candidate for U. S. Senate.

Persuasive essays are considered by many to be the supreme test of a writer's skill. Why? Because it requires reaching for a reader's head *and* heart, while presenting logical arguments in a style that's clear, interesting, winsome and reasonable. If you learn to do all that, there's nothing more I can teach you!

In this final section of *Wordsmith Craftsman*, you will learn how to define a position, think it through and present logical arguments in support of it. The goal is to persuade a reader to agree with you, but in the process you will probably find yourself thinking more clearly and deeply about your own convictions than ever before. You may even have to re-think some of them!

THE ELEMENTS OF PERSUASION

1. **Position.** The center of any persuasive essay is the position. This is a clear statement of the writer's opinion about a given topic. It is the ground, so to speak, that he or she is prepared to defend.

2. **Style** is important to all writing, but especially important in persuasive writing because more depends on it. If you want to convince, you'd better not bore or confuse. A clear, interesting style will keep the reader's attention while you present your case--and their attention is the one thing you must have, whether they end up agreeing with you or not.

3. **Tone.** The tone of a persuasive essay is the attitude that the writer seems to take. A piece may sound scholarly and rational in tone, or it may sound angry, humorous, melancholy, or ironic. Any of these could be effective, depending on the subject of the essay. But three tones to be avoided are sarcasm, portentousness, and flippancy.

a. *Sarcasm* is a cutting remark intended to wound or ridicule. It requires no skill or wit, and is often a shallow disguise for a shallow argument. Sarcasm also betrays a mean spirit in the writer; the very word is derived from the Greek for "biting the lips in rage." Alert readers may have detected a touch of sarcasm in the movie reviews on page 79. But what might be permissible in mocking a bad production is never persuasive. Sarcasm persuades no one. More often, it simply irritates.

b. *Portentousness.* A portentous tone is one in which the author tries to appear more profound than he actually is. The dictionary definition includes, "marked by pompousness; pretentiously weighty." Sweeping statements about the future are the hallmark of portentousness: "In ten more years, the rain forests will be gone." "Individual freedom in this country will soon disappear." Such pronouncements sound grand *only* to the writer, and those who already agree. Preachiness (lecturing the readers) and pretentiousness (pretending to have more learning than one really has) are similar mistakes in tone.

c. *Flippancy.* This is the opposite of portentousness; to be flippant is to take *nothing* seriously. Flippancy is out of place in any kind of writing, but especially when trying to be persuasive. When it is used to make an opposing view look trivial, it usually backfires: the writer is the one who ends up looking trivial.

An irritating tone will put off a reader even if your arguments are excellent, so consider your attitude carefully. The best "all purpose" tone is one of friendly reasonableness--earnest, but brightened with a touch of humor wherever appropriate.

4. **Argument.** This word probably conjures up a picture of a quarrel, punctuated perhaps by flying objects. But in persuasive writing, an argument is a reasoned statement (or collection of statements) made to prove the position. Below are five types of effective arguments:

a. *Common Ground* is the territory that a writer can assume his or her readers will share. Most of us would agree that peace is a more desirable condition than war, or that stable families are necessary for a stable society. Common ground isn't necessarily foolproof: some precepts of "what everybody knows" have come into question from time to time, and there are always a few "cranks" who question everything. But common assumptions of some sort are vital to any argument. Without them, we couldn't even begin.

b. *Legitimate authority.* Much of what we know, we accept on faith--because we were told by someone we trust. Our responsibility in argument is to be sure, first, that the authority we use is qualified to speak on the subject (such as a physicist on relativity theory or a highway commissioner on traffic safety) and second, that we represent his or her views accurately.

c. *Empirical Evidence.* Scientific studies, statistics, facts and figures can be very helpful in making your case. When using empirical evidence, be specific about how it was collected and what it proves. "Studies show . . ." is not convincing by itself.

d. *Personal experience* can be effective, but it is usually limited. For example, if you want to disprove the position that deaf people are slow learners, you may introduce your hearing-impaired-but-brilliant friend as evidence to the contrary. One case of brilliance, however, is not enough to prove anything, nor can you assume that your friend is typical. In most cases, you will need additional evidence.

e. *Logical reasoning.* Logic is a subject in itself; obviously we can't do much more than introduce it here. By now, however, you should have developed some capacity for logic, simply because you belong to a rational species. Logic is just one of the things people do--

although sometimes they don't bother to do it well. On pages 34-35, you encountered two words related to paragraph organization that also apply to well-known logical forms:

Inductive reasoning begins by assembling facts and using them to prove a position. For example: "Since numerous studies indicate that smoking increases the risk of lung cancer by 1000%, cigarettes should be banned now."

Deductive reasoning assumes a central fact or principle and shows specific examples of where it has led or will lead. For example: "Because smoking increases the risk of lung cancer by 1000%, Barbara is likely to contract cancer unless she quits now."

Logic can be especially useful in arguing for a situation that doesn't currently exist, as can

f. *Reasonable analogy*. An analogy is a comparison, which may be drawn from history, literature, or everyday life. For example: "Just as every household must balance its budget, the United States government is obliged to manage its finances prudently." For an analogy to be *reasonable* it must parallel your position at the crucial point you're trying to make. Even then, the use of analogy is limited; it can provide useful support, but shouldn't be your main argument.

Before trying your hand at persuasion, take a look at how other writers do it. Editorials are easy to find; though the Opinion pages of your local newspaper are an obvious first place to look, you can also search the web pages of political journals such as *National Review, The Nation, Reason, The Weekly Standard,* and *The New Republic*.

EXERCISE. Find an editorial in a newspaper or magazine and answer these questions about it:
1. What is the writer's position? (Express in one sentence, or find a thesis sentence in the article itself.)
2. What common ground, if any, does the author assume?
3. What sort of arguments does the author advance to make the case? (Try to find two.
4. Does the author try to engage the reader's sympathy? If so, how?
5. Is the tone of the piece appropriate, or offensive?

WRITING THE PERSUASIVE ESSAY

Students who participate in debating clubs are required to argue *both* sides of an issue with equal conviction--the goal of debate is argument itself. But the goal of persuasive writing (in this book, at least) is to use argument effectively to defend your personal convictions. We have spent a lot of time getting to it, but finally it's your turn.

ASSIGNMENT. Choose a belief that you hold strongly, and write a persuasive essay (1-2 double-spaced pages long) in support of it.

STEP ONE - THINK

Our society seems to have turned into a huge debating club, with all kinds of "hot button" issues tossed around in the media and everyday conversation. You probably have opinions about some of these issues. Your first task will be to choose one for your essay, and define your topic.

This will take us back to clustering. On a clean page in your notebook, and widely spaced so that you can cluster around them, write two subjects that you're concerned about. The subject does not necessarily have to be a burning social issue. The essay "How to Find Time" (see page 56) is persuasive, but it addresses an everyday problem.

You can only address one aspect of the issue in a single essay. Aspects of the abortion issue, for example, include its effect on society's moral base, the definition of "rights," the poor care provided at many clinics, the emotional nature of the debate, and so on. Each one of these could be detailed further. Select just one "branch" of the cluster as a topic for your essay.

Once you have the topic, write your thesis statement. In a persuasive essay, the thesis statement sets forth your position--the point you will defend. Don't rush this step! Your position must be limited to an area that you *can* defend in one or two pages, given your knowledge and your ability to think it all through before you even start writing.

Here are some examples of the progress from subject to topic to thesis statement (position):

```
Subject: Large families
Topic: Doubts about the CEI finding that children from
   large families do poorly in school.
Thesis statement: Although some resources are limited in
   large families, the main determining factor is the
   parents, not the number of children.

Subject: Lack of discipline in public schools
Topic: School uniforms as one way to enforce discipline
Thesis statement: By setting limits on the students while
   encouraging school spirit, uniforms would help create
   an atmosphere conducive to learning.

Subject: Raising the driving age to 18
Topic: Whether the presumed drop in highway fatalities
   would offset the hardships imposed on younger teens.
Thesis statement: Because the state has an obligation and
   a right to protect its citizens, raising the driving
   age might be justified.
```

Before going on to the organizing stage, you should have some idea how you will defend your position. List all the statements in favor of the position that you can support by legitimate authority, empirical evidence, personal experience, logic, reasonable analogy, or any combination. (We'll save the common ground statements for the next step.) Try to think of at least three arguments, and make sure that they all relate directly to your thesis statement. Be sure to verify any facts you will be presenting as empirical evidence.

EXAMPLES of appropriate arguments

LARGE FAMILIES ESSAY
Empirical evidence:
a. In the CEI report, other factors were not considered, such as income and immigrant status.
Logical reasoning:
b. Whether limited resources are a problem depend more on the parents than on the number of children.
Personal experience:
c. My personal survey of four large families proves that this need not be a problem.
(For this position, personal experience is effective; all the writer needs to do is prove that large families are not *necessarily* deprived of educational opportunity. Only one example is sufficient!)

SCHOOL UNIFORMS ESSAY
Logical reasoning:
a. School uniforms are a symbol of 1) limits and 2) expectations.
Empirical evidence:
b. Sacred Heart High School and Kensbury Prep (both low-income schools that require uniforms) boast high academic achievements.
Legitimate authority:
c. School years are a time for learning, not self-expression (quote from Dorothy Sayers).

STEP TWO - ORGANIZE

1. Determine your audience first; that will determine your common ground.

Each circle in the diagram below represents a different group. High school students hold certain concerns in common; parents, Christians, political liberals, and immigrants hold others. As you can see, many of these concerns overlap from one group to another, and there's tremendous variety within each group. All of them together might be classified as "law-abiding American citizens," a huge body that, though hard to define, nonetheless occupies some common ground. All law-abiding American citizens want a just society, value peace, and accept some standards of behavior.

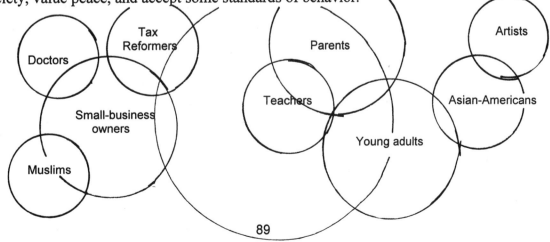

Write three or four assumptions that you believe your audience can accept. These won't necessarily appear in your essay, but they will help you define your arguments.

EXAMPLES of common ground

LARGE FAMILIES ESSAY
a. The family is a vital training ground for building relationships.
b. Parents determine family goals.
c. Spiritual goals have a higher priority than material goals.

SCHOOL UNIFORMS ESSAY
a. Learning is essential for success.
b. Discipline is necessary for learning.
c. A major problem in public schools today is discipline.

2. **To the best of your ability, anticipate the opponent's objections to your argument.**

No matter what your position is, someone is going to disagree with it: that's your opponent. To be as fair as possible, assume that your opponent is a man or woman of good will who holds his or her view sincerely. What arguments might such a person put up against your position? You've probably heard some of them already; if you were to imagine yourself in a verbal argument, you might even come up with more. Think of at least two common objections to your position, and write them down.

EXAMPLES of anticipated objections

LARGE FAMILIES ESSAY
a. The more children, the less money and time to go around.
b. Parents are usually overworked as it is.
c. The world is in danger of overcrowding.
(Crossed out because it does not relate to the thesis.)

SCHOOL UNIFORMS ESSAY
a. Stifles creativity; forces students to conform.
b. Not all can afford uniforms.
c. High academic ratings in private schools are a result of admissions policy, not uniforms.

3. **Organize your argument.**

By now you should have a lot of material to work with. Your task is to determine the best way to present it. The argument is the vehicle that will take your reader from the common ground to your specific position. We'll look at possible routes from one place to the other in a moment, but first let's discuss the role of feelings in persuasion.

THE PLACE OF EMOTION: Your main target is the reader's mind--you want to make him or her *think*. But without some heart involvement you will gain nothing more than assent; the reader may think, "Uh-huh. That makes sense"-- and promptly forget what you said. But if you touch the heart as well as the head, you've involved the whole person, and may even make a convert to your cause. You needn't be afraid to express deep feeling for the subject (as long as you're not abusive or overbearing about it). Personal examples and anecdotes can engage attention and sympathy while you illustrate a point. Emotional "arguments" can be effective, as long as you remember that "I feel" is never a substitute for "I can prove."

Here are three strategies for presenting an argument. All are sound; it's up to you to determine the best for your purposes.

a. Compare your strongest argument with your opponents'.
b. Start with what you consider to be your weakest argument and build up to the strongest.
c. Line up the major opposing arguments and demolish them by demonstrating their flaws: whether false evidence or invalid reasoning.

Once you've determined an approach that works for your arguments, write an outline for the essay. Include at least one real-life example in support of your position, drawn from your own experience or a reliable source.

EXAMPLES of strategy

LARGE FAMILIES ESSAY (using strategy "a")

```
    I. The California Study
   II. A Tale of two families
       A. The Petersons
          1. both parents work
          2. children unsupervised; discipline problems;
          poor  school performance
       B. Families participating in the California Study
          1. many immigrant and low-income families
          2. number of children not the only factor
       C. The Frankls
          1. mother at home, father involved in education
          2. homeschooling provides lots of interaction
          3. children learn to cooperate if they have to!
       D. Other large families I know
  III. Therefore--it all depends on the parents
       A. Values
       B. Commitment
   IV. Conclusion
```

SCHOOL UNIFORMS ESSAY (using strategy "c")

```
    I. The issue
   II. Objections (and answers)
       A. Private school can expel anyone they want to keep
       standards high (Example of two schools' expel rate)
       B. Many children can't afford uniforms.
```

>   1. Both schools help children raise the money.
>   2. "No student turned away."
>   C. School uniforms stifle creativity and individuality (answered in III)
> III. The real purpose of school: learning
>   A. Sayers quote
>   B. How to foster learning
>   1. teaching self-discipline
>   2. self-expression takes a back seat
> IV. How uniforms promote learning
>   A. Visible symbol of the school
>   1. school spirit
>   2. everyone engaged in the same enterprise
>   B. Eliminates a major distraction
>   1. Marcie the outrageous dresser
>   2. self-expression must be earned; not a right
> V. Conclusion

STEP THREE - WRITE

Write the body first, saving the introduction for later. Follow these guidelines:

1. Make your position clear in the first paragraph of the body.

2. Follow your outline.

3. Watch your tone! Don't allow yourself to become sarcastic, preachy, shrill, or anything else that will put off a reader.

4. Use humor (good-natured humor, that is) whenever possible, as long as it does not detract from the seriousness of the argument.

5. The conclusion should be a strong restatement of your position (though not in the same words), plus a challenge of some sort to the reader. What should the reader do? think? feel? Pay special attention to the last paragraph; can it be emphasized by long-short contrast, unusual word order, or parallel construction? (See pages 43- 45.)

When you're finished with the draft, consider possible introductory paragraphs. An effective introduction is vital for all types of essays, but especially for persuasive. You will use it as a "hook" to draw your reader, so that he or she will listen to what you have to say. Most of the techniques we've used so far can be adapted to a persuasive essay: the anecdote (or example), the quote, the foreshadowing statement. Another effective opening is the use of a startling fact or statistic to "wake up" the reader. Write two introductions, using two different techniques, then determine which one works best.

Finally, write a title for your essay. "Catchy" titles can attract readers that may not otherwise come your way, but if you can't think of anything clever, settle for something clear and straightforward.

STEP FOUR - EVALUATE

Since clarity *and* logic are equally important in a persuasive essay, you must judge the content carefully. That explains the longer list of evaluation questions. Read the questions first, and keep them nearby as you reread your essay.

1. Are you sure all terms will be understood by your readers as you intend?
2. Is your position stated promptly and clearly?
3. Do you make any assumptions that your readers may not share?
4. Are all your arguments valid? (That is, are all facts true, reasoning sound, authorities legitimate?)
5. Are the opposing arguments effectively answered?
6. Is the tone appropriate?
7. Does the introduction engage attention?
8. Does the conclusion state your position forcefully?

Once you're satisfied that your position is clear and well presented, check the essay against the style questions on pages 60-61.

Notice how the two sample essays that follow have presented their arguments. Compare with the outlines on pages 91-92.

LARGE FAMILIES, LARGE GOALS

"Children from large families typically perform poorly in school." This conclusion from a recent study by the California Education Institute made me see red for a moment. On second thought, I suppose this result would make sense to a lot of people: with more children, parents have less money and time to share around, right?

The study concludes that the number of children is the determining factor for poor school performance, although the data suggest other factors that may be just as crucial, such as low income or immigrant status. But the most important factor of all is hardly mentioned in the study: the parents' priorities.

The Petersons (not their real name) live in a big white frame house in our neighborhood. Both parents work to make the payments and feed their six children; often Mr. Peterson works overtime. The children are unsupervised from the time the school bus drops them off until Mrs. Peterson gets home from work. Because none of the children have been taught to do laundry or cooking chores, she has an entire evening of work ahead of her. Who has time to listen to reading lessons or talk to the kids about their day?

At the Frankl house (that's us!), seven children share three and a half bedrooms. Our house isn't as big as the Peterson's, but we can afford it on one salary: Dad's. Mom stays home--and so do the children. Because we're home-schoolers, we have lots of interaction with our parents. Even though my mother is very busy, she is always around to answer questions and spend time with each of us. Not only that, but we have been taught to help with <u>everything</u> around the house and assist each other with our chores. Somehow, housework and schoolwork get done, and the children are learning additional lessons in cooperation, patience, and helpfulness.

Is this unusual? Not in my experience. I personally know three other large families (four children or more) where the parents seem to have time for each child and the children perform well academically. Two are homeschooling families; one is not. The chief determining factor seems to be the parents.

Parents who are determined to provide time, training, and values for their children will find a way to do it. Their commitment will lead them to set priorities--make do with one car, invest in textbooks rather than gymnastics lessons, buy a smaller house--all so that one parent can stay home and teach the children the most important lesson they'll ever learn: how to live with others in loving relationships.

As far as I'm concerned the facts are in: parents with great goals will produce great results.

THE CASE FOR UNIFORMS IN SCHOOL

When the opening bells ring at Sacred Heart School and Kensbury Prep, the halls fill up with students hurrying to their first classes. The noise is continuous, but there's no shouting, no shoving, and least of all, no gunfire. That's not what the visitor will notice first thing, though. The most striking features of these students are their clean oxford shirts (pale blue at Sacred Heart, yellow at Kensbury), and dark slacks or skirts--the same for everyone.

School uniforms are coming into favor as a way to help solve the discipline problems that plague public education. Many private schools have required them for years, and uniforms obviously haven't hurt academic performance. Opponents claim that private schools may draw from the "cream of the crop" and expel any troublemakers to keep their academic ratings high. But Sacred Heart and Kensbury are prime examples to the contrary: both are located in lower-income neighborhoods, drawing kids who aren't usually expected to do well--yet Sacred Heart expelled only 2% of their students last year, and Kensbury even less.

Some object that low-income families cannot afford the uniforms, but both schools offer scholarship programs and fund-raising projects to pay for them. "No student is ever turned away for lack of money to buy a uniform," says Father James Ruble, Principal at Sacred Heart.

The strongest objection to school uniforms, however, is that requiring all students to dress alike stifles their individuality. To answer this, we must define the purpose of education. In a famous essay called "The Lost Tools of Learning," Dorothy Sayers wrote, ". . . the sole true end of education is simply this: to teach men how to learn for themselves; and whatever instruction fails to this is effort spent in vain." Self-expression doesn't accomplish this goal, but self-discipline does.

Uniforms promote discipline in at least two ways. First, they offer a visible symbol of the school and a continual reminder of what school is all about. All the students can see that they are involved in the same enterprise, and the uniform fosters a sense of school spirit. Second, uniforms eliminate a major distraction for students. When they are in school, they are supposed to be focused on learning, not on who's wearing what or how far to push the dress code. When I was in public school, one girl I knew was always making news with her "self-expression." Students sometimes placed bets on whether or not she would be sent to the principal's office because of the latest outrageous outfit--a big distraction from calculus! Of course, uniforms would not eliminate all distractions, but at least they would serve as a constant reminder of what school is for.

Self-expression is not necessarily a right; it is both learned and earned. Uniforms are a visible symbol of what learning is all about.

STEP FIVE - REWRITE

After all this work, you should consider sharing your essay. Does your local newspaper publish a forum for "young voices"? Do you know of an organization that publishes a newsletter about this issue? In a slightly shortened form, your essay would make an excellent letter to the editor, or perhaps your congressman should hear from you on the subject.

ASSIGNMENT. Send your persuasive essay to a publication or individual who would have an interest in the subject. Edit the essay, if necessary, to make it fit one page (typed and single-spaced).

ASSIGNMENT. Following Steps One through Five on pages 87-95, write another persuasive essay (2-3 pages long) on a topic that matters to you.

Notice that your next essay is to be a little longer. Not only will you be able to include more examples or anecdotes, but you should also be able to defend a broader position. Your position this time should include two main points, not just one; both adequately defined and defended.

To understand what I mean, consider our two sample essays in the previous section. "Large Families, Large Goals" defends the position that coming from a large family is not necessarily detrimental to high achievement in school. "The Case for School Uniforms" is longer because it addresses two lesser objections before taking on the main point: that school uniforms promote student training. We could expand both essays to encompass more than one main point. In the first essay, the position could be that children from large families: *a)* don't have to be deprived of their parents' time, and *b)* have a unique opportunity to learn valuable lessons in cooperation and patience. In the second essay, the additional point might be that school uniforms reduce pressure on students to dress like their peers.

In your thinking and organizing, you should come up with a little more of everything: more common ground statements, more opponents' objections, more valid arguments. In addition, you should give more time and thought to spotting any flaws in your reasoning. These flaws are called **fallacies of argument.**

On pages 108-110, you'll find a list of these fallacies presented in a handy chart form, so you can refer to them often. After you have written the statements in favor of your position at the end of Step One, consider each argument to check for fallacies. If any of your statements are flawed, rewrite it. Learning to recognize fallacies, as well as learning to avoid them, will sharpen your mind and make you unbeatable in debate!

THE VERSATILE WORDSMITH CRAFTSMAN

A "craftsman" in any field is one who is able to adapt his skills to a variety of circumstances and demands. As you continue to practice your writing, you should develop this same versatility--the ability to address a variety of subjects from many different angles. All it takes is practice.

> Choose two general subjects from the list on page 56 and write a descriptive, narrative, expository, and persuasive essay for *each* general subject (eight essays in all). For each essay, "cluster" a topic, write a thesis statement, and follow the steps as outlined in Part Three of this book. On pages 104-107, the steps for each type of essay are summarized for quick reference. Allow yourself two weeks for each narrative and descriptive essay, one month for each expository and persuasive essay--six months in all.

Once you've finished all eight essays and typed or printed them, put them together in a portfolio. Design a cover and a Table of Contents; if you are an artist or photographer, consider adding illustrations.

This collection is your "diploma" for the course--proof (if you've followed instructions) that you can handle language in many forms and for many purposes. You are able to communicate knowledge, ideas, and emotions. You can break down complex assignments and master them step by step. You will meet future demands with skills in hand that will make both thinking and writing much easier for you. In our world, that's worth a lot.

Congratulations!

NOTES ABOUT _____

Date: _____ Author/Speaker: _____ Source (title and page numbers):

_____

Abbreviations: _____

Main points: _____

_____

Notes: Observations:

_____

_____

_____

_____

_____

_____

_____

_____

_____

_____

_____

_____

_____

_____

_____

_____

_____

_____

_____

Your notes should include:
Specific information you don't already know   Important names, dates, places
Details that have significant consequences   Definitions of unfamiliar terms
Emphasized items, words, and concepts   Diagrams that help you understand
                                                     Questions about anything unclear to you

APPENDIX

SUMMARY OF _____

Date: _____ Author: _____ Source (title and page #):_____

Key words and phrases: _____

Skim the pages first, then determine the
Main point of the section: _____

_____

Mentally divide the material into 3-6 sections, assign a
title to each and use these titles as outline headings for the
General organization:

_____

_____

_____

Précis:

_____

_____

_____

_____

_____

_____

_____

_____

_____

_____

_____

_____

_____

_____

_____

Guidelines:
a. Stick to the essentials; concentrate on ideas rather than examples, details, or descriptions.
b. Add sentences, leading questions and other transitions to link the ideas in a way that shows their relationship.
c. Write a concluding sentence that pulls the main points together.

APPENDIX

ANSWERS FOR EXERCISES

Ex. A-1 (p. 30)
1. The Rhine is Europe's most picturesque and legendary river.
2. Trenton was the true turning point of the War.
3. It was a large lovely garden . . .
4. Nothing was visible, nor could be visible, to us, except straight lines.
5. Just making sure you were paying attention!
6. . . . things in general were settled forever.

Ex. A-2 (p. 31)
1. The warm summer evening is tranquil and nostalgic.
2. Christmas was coming, and Della had no money to buy a gift.
3. Socrates met his death with courtesy and dignity.
4. Our city's schools are in terrible shape.
5. Anticipation and apprehension characterize the dog show before judging begins.
6. (gasp!)

Ex. A-3 (p. 32)
1. The first sentence introduces a contrast ("but some of his conclusions are questionable") that the paragraph does not address.
2. The last sentence doesn't fit.
3. The second sentence inserts an expository note into what is essentially a description. It would work better at the beginning of the paragraph, but best in another paragraph altogether.
4. This paragraph has no focus. Too many ideas are introduced, and narrative, descriptive, expository and persuasive elements tangle with no clear winner.
5. This paragraph attempts to address two issues with equal weight. Is it about art, or television? The writer should choose one or the other.
6. Organization is the problem here. If the first sentence is the topic sentence, every other part of the paragraph should deal with the "starting crouch." The advice about shoes and watching the ball belongs elsewhere. Also, the paragraph should be arranged in a more logical order: finish the discussion of the racket before going on to the position of the feet.

Ex. B-1 (p. 37-38)
1. The gift delighted my brother.
2. Todd zoomed past the finish line.
3. One by one, guerrillas slipped by the guard post.
4. The prospect of going to Japan thrilled Rhoda.
5. Algebra infuriates me.

Ex. B-2 (p. 38)
1. Lower-income families feel neglected by government.
   (I didn't change government because in this case it's *supposed* to be impersonal.)
2. How many science professors teach at that school?
3. Clothing-industry executives want higher tariffs.
4. Congressmen have become detached and corrupt.
5. Our graduating seniors look forward to the future with anticipation.

Ex. B-3 (p. 39)
1. The "jump" scene was my all-time scariest moment at the movies.

2. The bystanders murmured to each other in monosyllables, some openly weeping.
3. In my junior year, I learned how to get the most from my reading.
4. The Omni-Sport is more likely than most compact cars to buckle on impact.
5. DataMax looks forward to increased sales as our products gain momentum this year.

Ex. B-4 (p. 39)
1. Saturday's game thrilled the fans.
2. The Rwandans desperately needed basic food supplies.
3. We would appreciate your prompt attention.
4. Thugs had broken the statue.
5. A busload of volunteers from the U. S. repaired the building.

Ex. B-5 (p. 40)
1. Her face fell and her lower lip trembled.
2. Mom shifted a little in her chair and coughed nervously.
3. Men without shoes and uniform jackets were wandering aimlessly, ignoring the orders of a flustered sergeant.
4. The unmistakable sound of low whispers and shuffling feet spread through the audience.
5. The children couldn't keep still; some were even jumping up and down.

Ex. B-6 (p. 41)
1. Treating customers rudely is the surest way to get fired.
2. With the temperature below zero, the men risked freezing to death.
3. She knows her mind. or, The woman knows her mind.
4. In case of a kitchen fire, customers will be evacuated quickly through the hotel lobby.
5. These are times that try men's souls.

Ex. B-8 (p. 42-43)
1. After 12 long weeks, Fred passed his EMT final exam. No more memorizing human anatomy terms or practicing life-saving techniques until 1:00 a.m. No more trying to sit upright and stay alert during afternoon classes. He admitted to himself that his certification was probably worth the effort, but it was an ordeal he hoped never to repeat.
2. Lewis Griffin was a veteran of 300 jumps. But when he made a routine jump out of a plane 13,000 feet over central Iowa, another diver accidentally crashed into him and knocked him unconscious. Suddenly Lew's experience meant nothing; he was hurtling toward the ground, arms flapping like a marionette's.
3. Every night, thousands of homeless men and women are sleeping on America's streets. The "system" has neglected the homeless, a fact that should trouble most of us. Should anything be done?

Essay questions (p. 56)
1. 1-N, 2-P, 3-N, 4-E, 5-E, 6-E, 7-P, 8-E, 9-P, 1O-P. The essay as a whole is Persuasive.
2. "Remember, most time is wasted in minutes, not hours." (#9)
4. Clear exposition of the problem; examples of well-spent time; Clement Moore story; suggestions for using time wisely
5. The inclusive words "most of us" (#1), which draw us into the problem; the familiar poem; the Clement Moore story (everybody likes stories!); examples we can relate to

DEWEY DECIMAL CLASSIFICATION SYSTEM

000 GENERAL WORKS
010 Bibliography
020 Library science
030 General encyclopedias
040 General collected essays
050 General periodicals
060 General societies, museums
070 Journalism
080 Collected Works
090 Rare books

100 PHILOSOPHY
110 Metaphysics
120 Metaphysical theories
130 Branches of psychology
140 Philosophic systems
150 Psychology
160 Logic
170 Ethics
180 Oriental, ancient philosophy
190 Modern philosophy

200 RELIGION
210 Natural religion
220 Bible
230 Doctrinal theology
240 Practical theology
250 Pastoral theology
260 Church theology
270 Church history
280 Christian churches and sects
290 Non-Christian religions

300 SOCIAL SCIENCES
310 Statistics
320 Political science
330 Economics
340 Law
350 Public administration
360 Social welfare
370 Education
380 Commerce
390 Customs

400 PHILOLOGY
410 Comparative philology
420 English language
430 Germanic language
440 French/Provincial
450 Italian/Rumanian
460 Spanish/Portuguese
470 Latin/Italic
480 Greek/Hellenic
490 Other languages

500 PURE SCIENCE
510 Mathematics
520 Astronomy
530 Physics
540 Chemistry, Mineralogy
550 Earth Sciences
560 Paleontology
570 Biological Sciences
580 Botany
590 Zoology

600 APPLIED SCIENCE
610 Medicine
620 Engineering
630 Agriculture
640 Home Economics
650 Business
660 Industrial Chemistry
670 Manufacturers
680 Mechanical Trades
690 Building

700 ARTS AND RECREATION
710 Landscape, Civic Art
720 Architecture
730 Sculpture
740 Drawing, Decorative Arts
750 Painting
760 Prints, Print Making
770 Photography
780 Music
790 Recreation

800 LITERATURE
810 American Literature
820 English Literature
830 German/Germanic Literature
840 French and Gallic Literature
850 Italian Literature
860 Spanish, Portuguese Literature
870 Latin/Italic Literature
880 Greek/Hellenic Literature
890 Other Literatures

900 HISTORY AND GEOGRAPHY
910 Geography/Travel
920 Biography
930 Ancient World History
940 European History
950 Asian History
960 African History
970 North American History
980 South American History
990 Oceania/Polar Regions

APPENDIX

SUMMARY OF STEPS IN ESSAY WRITING

DESCRIPTIVE ESSAYS

Descriptive essays may describe a person, place, or object. They tend to be short; some may be no longer than a paragraph. Descriptive essays are usually intended to provoke an emotional response.

ONE: THINK
1. Determine the purpose of the description (what response do you want from your reader?).
2. Write a thesis statement focusing on the aspect of your subject that you want to share.

TWO: ORGANIZE
1. Expand ideas in the thesis statement.
   Write a short list of examples, actions, memories.
   Write a list of sensory details: what you see, hear, smell, touch, and taste.
2. Reconsider the thesis statement; rewrite if necessary.
   Cross out any details that don't fit.
   Number ideas in a logical order.

THREE: WRITE
Guidelines:
1. Choose an organizing principle (see pages 33-36).
2. Include your thesis statement.
3. Make sure all sentences relate in some way to the thesis statement.
4. Include lots of detail

FOUR: EVALUATE
Content questions for descriptive essays:
1. Does the description succeed in its goal?
2. Is the organization logical?
3. Are any of the sentences confusing? too long? awkwardly put together?
4. Does every sentence relate in some way to the thesis statement?
5. Are there enough details to help the reader "see" the object of this description?
   (Continue with style questions on pages 60-61.)

FIVE: REWRITE

NARRATIVE ESSAYS

Narratives relate an action, experience, or sequence of events. A narrative essay usually reflects the experience of the writer. The purpose may be to arouse an emotional response, teach a lesson, illustrate a point, or entertain the readers.

ONE: THINK
1. Determine the purpose of your narrative.
2. Summarize the action in a few sentences.
3. Write a thesis statement that indicates your purpose.
4. Write a general thesis: a statement of universal application that relates to your purpose.

TWO: ORGANIZE
1. List the sequence of events in order; determine your focus.
2. List outstanding sensory details: what you saw, heard, smelled, touched, tasted.
3. Cross out unnecessary actions, events or details.

THREE: WRITE
Guidelines:
1. Include enough background material to let the reader understand the setting.
2. Use strong action verbs whenever possible.
3. Include sensory details to give the reader a sense of "being there."
4. Include at least one direct quote or brief dialogue.
5. At the beginning or end, make it clear how your experience relates to some universal principle or application. You may or may not choose to use your thesis statement.

When the body of the narrative is completed, write an introductory paragraph (see page 107).

FOUR: EVALUATE
Content questions for narrative essays:
1. Is the narrative interesting, clear, and understandable?
2. If not,
    a. check the sequence to be sure you told everything in order.
    b. Add any time or space transitions to help explain the action.
    c. Add any details or linking sentences that would fill the gaps in understanding.
3. Are any of the sentences confusing? too long? awkwardly put together?
4. Are there enough concrete details to allow the reader to enter the action?
5. Is the purpose or application clear?
    (Continue with style questions.)

FIVE: REWRITE

EXPOSITORY ESSAYS

Expository writing is factual; its purpose is to inform. Expository *essays* are written chiefly to inform as well, but allow room for personal touches, such as the writer's observations and feelings, humorous asides, and statements of opinion.

ONE: GATHER INFORMATION
1. Read a general article on the subject; choose a topic narrow enough to discuss adequately.
2. Write a tentative thesis statement (you may change it later when you have more information).
3. Obtain further information from print sources, oral sources, or personal experience.
4. Determine the purpose of your essay (yes, it's to inform, but to inform about *what*, specifically?).

TWO: ORGANIZE
1. Once you have all the information you need, revise your thesis statement, if necessary.
2. Ask yourself what a reader would like to know about this topic.
3. Make an outline showing the direction you will go and the specific areas you will address.

THREE: WRITE
Guidelines:
1. Follow your outline.
2. Use at least one direct quote from a print or oral source.
3. Make no general statements, except in conclusion; all your information should be specific.
4. Add interest by using personal experiences, specific examples, or anecdotes (wherever appropriate).
5. Summarize your main point(s) about the topic in the last paragraph.
Write an introductory paragraph (see suggestions on page 107).

FOUR: EVALUATE
Content questions for expository essays:
1. Does it make sense and flow logically?
2. Are all direct quotations cited (that is, did you explain where you got the quote)?
3. Are all facts (names, dates, sequences, etc.) correct?

4. Is the essay interesting? If not, would further examples or illustrations help?
5. Does your introduction create interest in the topic? Would you want to finish the essay, after reading only the introduction?
    (Continue with style questions.)

FIVE: REWRITE

CRITICAL ESSAYS

Critical essays fall in two categories. One is the *review*, which is a writer's evaluation of a recent book, movie, theater production, art exhibit, concert or music CD. The second category is an exploration of a particular aspect of, or question regarding, any of the same, whether recent or classical. (The following steps apply primarily to a review.)

ONE: THINK
1. Make a checklist (written or mental) of qualities appropriate to the kind of work.
2. As you watch, read, or listen to the work in question, evaluate how it measures up to your standards.
3. Consider what the "message" of the work might be, and how that message is communicated.
3. Feel free to compare the work to others like it that you consider excellent.

TWO: ORGANIZE
1. Decide whether your overall reaction is negative or positive.
2. List specific reasons why you came to that conclusion.
3. List examples from the work itself that support your reasons.

THREE: WRITE
Guidelines:
1. In the first paragraph, explain briefly what the movie, play or book is about, giving some indication of your overall opinion of it. Do not bog down in details of the plot.
2. In the next paragraphs, give specific reasons for your opinion.
3. Use specific examples to support your reasons; don't just make a list of qualities, good or bad.
4. Sum up your opinion in the last paragraph, making it clear whether the work should be patronized or avoided.

FOUR: EVALUATE
Content questions for critical essays:
1. Do you still agree with your judgment, or would you change a few minor points?
2. Is there enough information to inform the reader what the work is about?
3. Does the plot summary contain irrelevant details?
4. Is the focus on one or two major criticisms or does this review threaten to become a list?
5. Is your opinion supported with evidence from the production itself?
    (Continue with style questions.)

FIVE: REWRITE

PERSUASIVE ESSAYS

Persuasive writing is designed to provoke a response from the reader. The most effective persuasive essays are designed to reach the head by way of the heart; in other words, they present factual and logical arguments in a winning way.

ONE: THINK
1. "Cluster" your subject (or narrow in some other way) to get a manageable topic.
2. Write a thesis statement expressing the main point you wish to defend or prove.

3. List statements in favor of your position. Make sure you can support these statements by personal experience, empirical evidence, legitimate authority, reasonable analogy, or logical reasoning. Check for fallacies (see pages 108-110).

TWO: ORGANIZE
1. Determine your common ground. Write 2-3 assumptions you believe your audience will accept.
2. Anticipate the opponent's objections to your argument.
3. Organize your argument. Some possibilities:
   a. Compare your strongest argument with your opponents'.
   b. Start with your weakest argument, and build up to the strongest.
   c. Line up the major opposing arguments, and demolish them one by one.
4. Write an outline for your essay.

THREE: WRITE
Guidelines:
1. State your position in the first paragraph of the body (not the introductory paragraph).
2. Follow your outline.
3. Be sure that your tone will not put off the reader (no sarcasm, preachiness, fury, etc.).
4. Use humor when appropriate.
5. Make your conclusion a strong restatement of your position that moves the reader to a response.
Write an introductory paragraph (see suggestions below).

FOUR: EVALUATE
Content questions for persuasive essays:
1. Are you sure all terms will be understood as you mean them to be understood?
2. Is your position stated promptly and clearly?
3. Do you make any assumptions that your readers may not share?
4. Are all your arguments valid (facts true, reasoning sound, authorities legitimate)?
5. Are opposing arguments dealt with fairly?
6. Is the tone appropriate?
7. Does the introduction engage a reader's attention?
8. Does the conclusion state your position forcefully?
   (Continue with style questions.)

FIVE: REWRITE

SUGGESTIONS FOR INTRODUCTORY PARAGRAPHS

Some of these suggestions are especially appropriate for narrative, some for expository, some for persuasive. It's a good idea to write more than one introductory paragraph for the same essay, then determine which works best.
* Begin with a quote.
* Begin with a foreshadowing statement.
* Begin in the middle of the action.
* Begin with a little-known (or shocking) fact, example, or statistic.
* Relate a brief anecdote which illustrates the main point of the essay.
* Relate a personal experience relevant to the topic.
* Comment briefly from an unusual point of view.
* Ask a question or a series of questions.

COMMON FALLACIES OF ARGUMENT

A **fallacy of argument** is a mistake in reasoning. Sometimes it's a deliberate "mistake"--a diversionary tactic that draws attention away from the real issue, a smokescreen that obscures the argument. Some fallacies are honest but not well thought-out, such as the *non sequitur*--a conclusion that does not logically follow from the points already made. Most fallacies are presented with a straight face, so to speak--so smoothly and convincingly that many readers don't catch them. But you must learn to recognize fallacies, not only to avoid them in your own writing but also to be aware of them when they appear in print.

1. **Fallacies of distraction** attempt to sidestep the argument by diverting the reader's attention. This can be done in a number of ways:

DEFINITION OF FALLACY	EXAMPLES	EXPLANATION OF ERROR
a. *Ad Hominem*. The Latin term means "toward the person." An *ad hominem* "argument" is really an attack on those who hold a certain position, rather than on the position itself. In its worst form, it sinks to mere name-calling and stirs up a cloud of anger in which the true merits or shortcomings of the position are lost.	Only trigger-happy rednecks support gun control. Only bleeding-heart liberals support gun control.	*These are very obvious examples, but most ad hominem arguments are easy to spot. The distraction is to associate one side of the issue (the "wrong" side) with unsavory characters or unacceptable views.*
b. "Poisoning the Well" is very similar to *ad hominem*. This is an attempt to invalidate the opposing view because individuals who hold that view don't come up to a standard set by the writer.	I've never met a single pro-life activist who adopted one of those babies he was trying to "save."	*It may be true that the writer has never met a pro-lifer who adopted, but what does that have to do with the pros and cons of abortion?*
c. *Ad populum*. This is an appeal "to the people" and anything held dear by the public at large. Revered figures such as Abraham Lincoln, as well as time-honored symbols like the flag are often enlisted in support of a cause-- sometimes even on opposite causes, as in this example:	No principle was dearer to our founding fathers than the separation of church and state. Our founding fathers, who under-stood the importance of morality, established a Christian nation.	*There is nothing wrong with presenting the views of the founding fathers. But in these examples, the "founding fathers" are being waved like a flag. We can be sure they didn't all believe the same thing! This would be more convincing if one or two individuals were named, and quoted.*
d. *Ad misicordiam* is an appeal to sympathy. The writer hopes we will side with an object worthy of our pity or respect.	Only a fanatic with a heart of stone would refuse an abortion to this poor 13-year-old runaway. My grandfather worked every day of his life, even when he was sick, and never asked for a handout.	*In the first example, a "worst-case scenario" is used to drum up support. In the second, we are expected to side with proud, hardworking ancestors against those who are looking for a free lunch.*
e. The *genetic* fallacy is the attempt to trace one's conviction back to a personal prejudice or some other shortcoming.	Homophobes use religion as an excuse for their anti-gay bias. Liberals spout "compassion" as a way to get power.	*In each of these examples, the writer refuses to admit that opposing views can be held sincerely or for legitimate reasons.*

f. *Ipse dixit* means "he said it himself." This is an attempt to shore up an argument by appealing to an authority that the reader would (presumably) respect. The fallacy here lies in holding up an authority who may not be qualified to make a judgment on the issue at hand

Even William F. Buckley, an acknowledged conservative icon, believes that drugs should be legalized.

Religion is inherently irrational. Karl Marx called it "the opiate of the masses."

If the writer wishes to prove that some conservatives support drug legalization, the first example is valid. If he's using it to prove that drugs should be legalized, it's inadequate--Mr. Buckley is not a doctor or drug expert. Nor was Karl Marx a theologian or psychologist.

---

2. **Fallacies of logic** deal with the argument itself.

DEFINITION OF FALLACY	EXAMPLE	EXPLANATION OF ERROR
a. *Equivocation* means using terms carelessly. Words can have different meanings in different contexts: a writer who uses the word as if it meant the same thing in all cases will only succeed in confusing the issue.	All religions exhort us to "Love our neighbor." What kind of love would withhold food from the children of welfare mothers?	*The word "love" has at least eight dictionary meanings and any number of personal meanings. But the writer does not define the word, and thus appears to equate a general religious principle with supporting government welfare.*
b. *Begging the question* is asking the reader to accept an unproven assumption as an argument. All arguments begin with some assumptions: the common ground. But a writer who begs the question is trying to slip in an unproven assumption "disguised" as common ground.	The only way humanity can escape certain disaster is to take charge of the next stage of evolution, beginning with stem-cell research. How can anyone think of abolishing the Department of Education when American schools are performing worse then ever?	*This statement assumes there was a **first** stage of evolution.* *This statement assumes a connection between the Department of Education and quality schools.*
c. *Over-generalizing* is drawing a broad conclusion from a small body of evidence. A writer's personal experience is usually insufficient evidence for coming to a conclusion; so is a single study or a limited statistic.	At least two cases of rottweilers attacking children have been documented in our city. These are truly vicious dogs. The American bald eagle is disappearing. Officials report a 10% drop in sighting at Willow Branch wildlife refuge.	*In each statement, only one bit of evidence is given to support the assertion a) that rottweilers are vicious and b) that the bald eagle is nearing extinction. Much more is needed to make the case that there is a problem and something should be done.*
d. The *either/or* dilemma presents only two options for the reader, one of them obviously disagreeable. The fallacy lies in over-simplifying the issue.	Students who don't prepare for college may as well prepare for a "career " of pumping gas. If we don't start enforcing strict environmental protection now, our planet will become a parking lot.	*Options for non-collegians may be limited, but they extend far beyond the gas station. Likewise, there may be other means of preserving the environment besides strict government regulation.*

e. The *Post hoc* fallacy relates to cause and effect. It assumes that something which occurred before a given result was the direct cause of that result. A *post hoc* assumption *may* be true, but more evidence is needed to prove it.

Raising taxes in the early 1990s gave us a booming economy.

Kim would never have gotten into drugs if she hadn't gone to college.

Other factors probably play an equal or greater part in the booming economy and in Kim's drug problem. These other factors should at least be acknowledged.

---

f. A *false analogy* is a misleading comparison--misleading because the comparison differs from the real-life issue at a critical point. Even accurate analogies, though helpful for explaining or illustrating a concept, should never be put forward as sole proof.

The death penalty is like a lighthouse, warning potential murderers away from the certain consequence of their crimes.

Would you send your children into artillery fire? Then why send them to public school?

Lighthouses warn honest sailors, not criminals. "Potential murderers" may not be honest enough to heed a warning.

Some public schools can indeed be dangerous, but "artillery fire" overstates the case and mars your claim to reasonableness.

---

g. *Non sequitur* literally means, "it does not follow. A non sequitur makes an inference or draws a conclusion from statements that have no logical connection to that inference or conclusion.

If we really cared about the homeless we would stop spending millions on defense.

Those who criticize the protestors apparently don't have much respect for free speech.

What's the logical connection between defense money and the homeless?

If "free speech" means the right to protest, doesn't it also mean the right to be critical of the protestors?